THE DIARY OF JAMES T. AYERS

THE FOLLOWING PAGE—A FACSIMILE OF A PAGE IN THE DIARY—SHOWS JAMES T. AYERS. UNDER THE PORTRAIT HE HAS WRITTEN "JOSEPH TAKE CARE OF THEASE TILL I COME HOME IF I EVER DO. THIS I HAD DREW BY I. H. PHILLIPS THAT BUNKS WITH ME. HE IS FROM FAIRBURY." A DIFFERENT VERSION OF THE POEM ABOVE THE PORTRAIT IS PRINTED ON PAGE 109.

He looks oald fashioned Gray and toughf,
sure in the lamp is Just the place
To draw the Squires Long fine face

the verse Above   I composed
                              my self

here
is ...st
Black
men
...
...ldan

April
vol infan
at Bridg...

Joseph take care of these till I come
home if ever I do this I had drawn
...Phelps that thinks...

THE DIARY OF JAMES T. AYERS

Civil War Recruiter

Edited, with a New Preface,

by

JOHN HOPE FRANKLIN

With a New Introduction

by

JOHN DAVID SMITH

LOUISIANA STATE UNIVERSITY PRESS
Baton Rouge

Louisiana Paperback Edition, 1999
08 07 06 05 04 03 02 01 00 99
5 4 3 2 1

Library of Congress Cataloging-in-Publication Data
Ayers, James T., 1805–1865.
    The diary of James T. Ayers, Civil War recruiter / edited, with a
new preface, by John Hope Franklin : with a new introduction by John
David Smith. —Louisiana paperback ed.
        p.   cm.
    Originally published: Springfield : Printed by authority of the
State of Illinois, 1947.
    Includes index.
    ISBN 0-8071-2393-5 (alk. paper)
    1. Ayers, James T., 1805–1865 Diaries. 2. United States—History—
Civil War, 1861–1865—Participation, Afro-American. 3. United
States—History—Civil War, 1861–1865 Personal narratives.
4. United States. Army—Recruiting, enlistment, etc.—Civil War,
1861–1865. 5. Clergy—Illinois—Diaries. I. Franklin, John Hope,
1915–   II. Title.
E540.N3A96   1999
973.7'8—dc21   99-14272
                                                                   CIP

CONTENTS

ILLUSTRATIONS

PREFACE

When I discovered the diary of James T. Ayers in the library of St. Augustine's College in 1943, I was pleased to edit it for publication in 1947. At the time, interest in the role of African Americans in the Civil War was just entering a stage of renewal. There had been several major works in the field in the generation following the war. Joseph T. Wilson's *Black Phalanx* appeared in 1882, while George Washington Williams's *History of the Negro Troops in the War of the Rebellion* and William Wells Brown's *The Negro in the American Rebellion* came out six years later. These books were followed in 1891 by Luis F. Emilio's *History of the Fifty-Fourth Regiment of Massachusetts Volunteer Infantry.* The long hiatus between these studies and the publication of the Ayers diary was interrupted early by briefer accounts in the *Journal of Negro History* and casual references to this or that aspect of individual or regimental service. The two exceptions were Bell Wiley's *Southern Negroes, 1861–1865* and Herbert Aptheker's *The Negro in the Civil War,* both of which appeared in 1938 and provided extensive and important evaluations of African American experience—both civilian and military—during the war years.

With the publication of Benjamin Quarles's *The Negro in the Civil War* in 1953, a new era in African American Civil War historiography began. It was followed in 1956 by *The Sable Arm: Negro Troops in the Union Army* by Dudley T. Cornish. By that time, thanks to these pioneer works as well as a wider recognition of the part Africans played in the history of the United States, subsequent Civil War studies generally included African Americans to a greater extent. A signal recognition of this trend was the work that emerged in 1965 from the distinguished historian James McPherson, *The Negro's Civil War: How American Negroes Felt and Acted During the War for the Union.*

Thus, the trend toward inclusiveness in the writing of United States history was perhaps better reflected in Civil War history than in other periods. In 1982, *The Black Military Experience* by Ira Berlin, Joseph P. Reidy, and Leslie S. Rowland appeared, followed in 1990 by Joseph T. Glatthaar's *Forged in Battle: The Civil War Alliance of Black Soldiers and White Officers.* Indeed, the services of African American soldiers and sailors have come to be celebrated even more enthusiastically in recent years, with the refurbishing and rededication of Augustus Saint-Gaudens's Robert Shaw Memorial on Boston Common in 1983, and the prominent positioning in 1997 of a panel from that memorial in the National Gallery of Art. Finally, in Washington in July 1998, there was the unveiling of the Memorial to African American Civil War soldiers, with a large number of descendants of those soldiers present, some wearing the regimental colors and medals of their ancestors. The event occurred precisely a century and a decade after George W. Williams had suggested such a memorial in his *History of the Negro Troops in the War of the Rebellion*.

James T. Ayers could not possibly have foreseen how significant his modest role would come to seem, and surely he could not have imagined or understood the increasing attention and even appreciation these recruits would receive down through the years. One would hope that, if possible, he would have seen such recognition as a part of the evolving democracy to which he, and they, contributed so much.

INTRODUCTION TO THE 1999 EDITION

John David Smith

In 1983, while browsing in a used book shop, I stumbled upon an unassuming little edition with the following words printed in small letters on its spine: "Ayers Diary/Franklin/Publication No. 50." I took a quick glance at the title page and discovered that the "Franklin" in fact was the esteemed historian John Hope Franklin, and after a further look at the contents, I concluded that this was the diary of a white lay preacher who recruited African American troops during the Civil War, a topic long of interest to me. I bought the book immediately, delighted to have it for my research, but nonetheless annoyed that I was unfamiliar with an account edited by perhaps the leading scholar in my field. How could I have missed it? Through the years I learned that while a few specialists had cited *The Diary of James T. Ayers, Civil War Recruiter* in their work, most Civil War historians were unaware of Franklin's short book published in 1947.

Several factors explain the diary's relative obscurity. First, scholars at the time generally had little interest in the role of African Americans in the Civil War. Even today, when slavery and emancipation studies rank among the best of our scholarship on the war, the mechanics of the recruitment of the almost 180,000 men who joined the U.S. Colored Troops remains largely undocumented and unexplored. Second, the provenance of Franklin's edition also explains its fugitive quality. Originally issued in a special edition as part of the Illinois State Historical Society's Occasional Publications, the book received limited attention from professional historians beyond the society's membership. Third, until recently many historians questioned the reliability and importance of diaries and other primary sources left by semiliterate non-elites like the Illinois farmer and itinerant minister James T. Ayers (1805–1865). Two decades after the book's publication, for example, James I. Robertson, Jr., brushed Franklin's edition aside as "a rambling, disjointed diary by an elderly anti-slaveryite who served in the 129th Illinois and as a recruiter for Negro units; the narrative spans only the last eighteen months of the war in the West."[1] But fortunately times and tastes have changed. Today the subject of African Americans in the Civil War era is of central interest to an increasingly large number of mainstream scholars who find new meaning in reading a variety of hitherto ignored texts.

Years before the start of the Civil Rights revolution, and decades before scholars focused intensely on blacks in the Civil War, Franklin, who received his Ph.D. from Harvard in 1941, recognized the historical value of Ayers's diary. He discovered it in the library of St. Augustine's College in Raleigh, North Carolina, having taught there (1939–1943) before moving to North Carolina College in Durham (1943–1947), now North Carolina Central University, and then to Howard University. Franklin already had published his definitive *The Free Negro in North Carolina, 1790–1860* in 1943, and four years later he wrote what was destined to become his best known book, *From Slavery to Freedom: A History of Negro Americans*. In 1947 Franklin also published an award-winning essay on Ayers as a recruiting agent of black troops. Because the Illinois State Historical Society considered Ayers's diary "so unique and entertaining," the society decided to issue the text in book form for its members.[2] Later that year, after Franklin had joined the Howard faculty, *The Diary of James T. Ayers, Civil War Recruiter* appeared. It was Franklin's first edited book.

Though Ayers's diary had a limited distribution and thus received relatively little attention from future historians, contemporary reviewers awarded it high marks. Fred A. Shannon, an expert on Civil War recruiting, praised Franklin's edition "as an illustration of the cultural level of western lay preachers." Ayers's observations of secessionists, their slaves, and his contempt for commissioned officers, according to Henry L. Swint, an authority on ex-slave contrabands, "have an authentic ring and a spicy flavor which makes his diary

1. Allan Nevins, James I. Robertson, Jr., and Bell I. Wiley, eds., *Civil War Books: A Critical Bibliography* (2 vols.; Baton Rouge: Louisiana State University Press, 1967), I, 53. In his classic *The Sable Arm: Negro Troops in the Union Army, 1861–1865* (New York; Longmans, Green, 1956), 326, Dudley Taylor Cornish considered the Ayers diary "of value for its discussion of the problems of Northern state recruiting agents in the Deep South during the Civil War."

2. "Historical News and Notices," *Journal of Southern History* 13 (May 1947): 292; Franklin, "James T. Ayers, Civil War Recruiter," *Journal of the Illinois State Historical Society* 40 (September 1947): 267–97 (quotation on page 267n). Franklin's article received second prize in the Alfred W. Stern contest for essays on Illinois or Illinoisans in the Civil War.

valuable as an indication of the midwestern Yankee as he came into contact with the South." And Frank Freidel, a careful student of Civil War intellectual history, praised Ayers's eclectic diary as a work of "unsophisticated candor," one that offered "another glimpse of the Civil War through the far from acute eyes of one of the ordinary people." Ironically, Freidel noted, "the extreme mediocrity" of Ayers's text accounted for "its considerable significance. It presents the war as it must have appeared to countless Northerners."[3]

As Franklin explains in his useful introduction, Ayers was a native Kentuckian who, after settling with his family in Ohio, moved westward to Illinois in 1831. Vehemently antislavery and patriotic in his sentiments, he was a restless backwoods crusader who harbored no love for the South in general or for white southerners in particular. Like other antislavery Republicans, Ayers believed that the "ungodly Southern Slave drivers and Slave breeders . . . [had conspired] to spread there unholy and monstrous sistom of making merchandise of Human soals" (26). Fully convinced of the "slave power conspiracy," he held white southerners and their "peculiar institution" responsible for the war and vowed that they should not be allowed to topple the Union that the Founding Fathers had sacrificed so much to construct. Sympathetic to the slaves, Ayers described them as "an ignorant people and how Could they be otherwise. We should perhaps be but Little better if Plaiced in there Position. Educate them, set good Examples before them. Let them know they are men and women and are A part and parcel of Gods Creation and I feel Sambo will do tolerably well" (50). Emancipation, Ayers insisted, would be God's will.

But like many white northerners who opposed slavery, Ayers considered persons of African descent inherently backward and inferior. He consistently referred to them as things, a commodity worth "geathering up" (6, 8). While he blamed slavery for the Negro's degradation and sympathized with the slaves' plight, Ayers nonetheless shared the racial phobias of his day. "Dam the niggers," he wrote in September 1864, reacting to commonly held fears that exslaves would migrate northward and marry white women. "I would Rather Blow there Brains out than they should do this," he stated. "No man would abhor the sight of A big buck nigger leading my daughter or Any white mans

3. Reviews by anonymous in *Missouri Historical Review* 43 (January 1949): 183–84; Shannon in *American Historical Review* 53 (April 1948): 630; Swint in *Journal of Southern History* 14 (May 1948): 279–80; Freidel in *Mississippi Valley Historical Review* 35 (May 1948): 320–21.

Daughter Round than I and yet I think we have ungrounded fears" (50). Though antiblack slurs abound in his diary, Ayers's repeated expressions of outrage over the April 12, 1864, massacre of black troops at Fort Pillow, Tennessee, suggest he had no personal malice toward African Americans. His was the crude, unvarnished racism of an antislavery Republican, an uneducated man who lived in cultural isolation along the Illinois frontier.

It was in fact his devotion to Illinois and to the Union, not his concern for blacks, that led the nearly fifty-seven-year-old Methodist Episcopal itinerant minister in September 1862 to abandon his second wife, lie about his age, and enlist in Company E, 129th Illinois Volunteer Infantry. "They say my Country needs me," Ayers wrote, "and I am willing to forego all this and even more if need be to save my Country. My life is ready if need be to Lay on the alter of my Country . . . everything I have . . . and more had I more, for my Country" (25–26). By July 1863 he was on detached service and assigned to recruit Negro troops in Tennessee under Military Governor Andrew Johnson. Having proven himself successful in this work (he recruited over two hundred men, for example, in Gallatin, Tennessee), on December 25, 1863, Ayers received an appointment, with the rank of private, as recruiting agent for the U.S. Colored Troops.[4] He began his duties and his diary three days later in Stevenson, Alabama.

Ayers recruited black troops in northern Alabama, many of whom served in the 17th U.S. Colored Infantry until October 1864, and his diary remains one of our best firsthand accounts of enlisting blacks in towns and on plantations. Though at times naive and bungling in his attempts to convince blacks to join the army, Ayers nevertheless was reasonably successful, especially when he had armed black soldiers to assist him. In his article, Franklin explained Ayers's method:

> After a town had been taken by Union forces, Ayers would move in and proceed to enlist Negro recruits. He would nail up attractive posters provided by the Ad-

4. On the activities of recruiting agents in Tennessee and northern Alabama, see *Freedom: A Documentary History of Emancipation, 1861–1867*, Series II, *The Black Military Experience*, eds. Ira Berlin, Joseph P. Reidy, and Leslie S. Rowland (Cambridge: Cambridge University Press, 1982), 122–26, 172–82. On overall recruitment policies and procedures, see Joseph T. Glatthaar, *Forged in Battle: The Civil War Alliance of Black Soldiers and White Officers* (New York: Free Press, 1990), 61–80. On blacks in Civil War combat, see Noah Andre Trudeau, *Like Men of War: Black Troops in the Civil War, 1862–1865* (Boston: Little, Brown, 1998).

jutant General's office and then would announce a meeting at which he would speak. If he succeeded in assembling a number of Negroes, he would appeal to them along two lines. In the first place, he would impress on his hearers the importance of getting into the fight in order to extend the blessings of liberty to their more unfortunate brothers who were still enslaved. Then he would tell them that the ten dollars per month, food, and clothing would give them some semblance of security and independence.

In rural areas, Ayers asserted that he frequently was the first to inform slaves in Confederate-held territory of their freedom under the Emancipation Proclamation. This occurred, for example, as late as May 1864, at the Eldridge plantation near Huntsville, Alabama.[5]

Recruiting was difficult work, as Ayers complained repeatedly in his diary. He often encountered what Franklin described as "the stern resistance of white men or women who branded him as an inciter of trouble and one who interfered with the peace and happiness of the slaves." In one instance, after Ayers had engaged in a heated exchange with the daughter of an Alabama planter, the woman, after insulting him, said, "I want you always to know sir I hait you in my verry Hart." To this Ayers replied, "Your are A disgrace to the sects [sex]. Shame on you Siss" (32–33). The recruiter then entered the woman's house and signed up four of her slaves for the 15th Tennessee Colored Regiment.

While opposition by white southerners was to be expected, Ayers found surprising the initial reluctance and the lack of enthusiasm by the slaves and ex-slaves to join the U.S. Colored Troops. He complained frequently that the blacks offered all manner of excuses not to enlist. And though a zealous recruiter in what Ayers considered to be a holy war against slavery, he gradually became disappointed and disillusioned by the slow recruiting process. Writing, for example, on September 7, 1864, Ayers remarked that he was "hartily sick of Coaxing niggers to be Soaldiers Any more. They are so trifleing and mean the[y] dont Deserve to be free" (46). Having said this, Ayers still believed that "Perhaps I have in this way [as a recruiter of black troops] been of more service to my Country than in Any other way I could have been imployed, so all write" (47). And despite his impatience with the slaves he encountered, he never lost faith in the importance of their emancipation. "Those that have got out from under master are," Ayers observed, "According to there Chance, making

5. Franklin, "James T. Ayers, Civil War Recruiter," 278–79.

good crops of Corn and Cotton and seem to be striving to do as best they can" (49). But eventually the rigors of his work wore Ayers down. On September 13 he resolved that "I am so tired of nigger Recruiting I am going as soon as A train goes through to Nashville to Resign and Go back to my Reg. or try" (54).

In October 1864, Ayers finally resigned his appointment and rejoined his old outfit, the 129th Illinois Volunteer Regiment. He participated in rear-guard actions as General William T. Sherman's army made its way northward through Georgia and the Carolinas in the last months of the war. Soon after Appomattox, Ayers took stock of the war's meaning, remarking "thank God . . . this Cruel war is over and I trust A permanent Peace is made. Having knocked the nigger out of thos ungodly Traitors and taught them A Lesson they nor there Children nor there Childrens Children will never forget that being Southerners dont necessarily make them better than other men" (98).

In addition to his descriptions of the recruiting process, Ayers's diary includes many penetrating observations of social and religious life in military camps, the presidential election of 1864, the destruction of Confederate civilian and military property by Union troops, and the soldiers' response to President Abraham Lincoln's assassination. Though Ayers wrote his last diary entry on May 24, 1865, he continued in the military, obtaining a commission first as chaplain, and then as first lieutenant, of the 104th U.S. Colored Troops. Sick and often incapacitated during his service, Ayers died of typhus in a military hospital while with his regiment in South Carolina in September 1865.

In editing Ayers's diary, Franklin provides a succinct introduction, including a clear statement of his editorial method and the manuscript's provenance. He arranged the entries in chronological order and made only minor emendations to clarify Ayers's intent. As is obvious from the excerpts quoted here, Franklin employed the literal method to transcribe the original text, thereby retaining most of Ayers's original spelling, capitalization, and punctuation and thus enhancing the text's sense of time and place. The editor also provides useful in-text information that indicates Ayers's location at the time of writing entries. It is especially noteworthy that in this edition, researched more than a half century ago, Franklin was one of the first scholars to employ Civil War veterans' pension records and documents of the Bureau of Colored Troops at the National Archives. These are essential records today for any serious student of the recruitment and use of black troops and the entire emancipation process.

In sum, readers will welcome the availability of this new edition of Ayers's "rambling, disjointed diary," ably edited by John Hope Franklin in 1947, while he was still launching his distinguished career. They will find Ayers's text an extremely valuable document, one that illumines the process of recruiting black soldiers as Union armies enveloped the war-torn South and describes the action and attitudes of civilians, white and black, caught in their path. Significantly, Franklin's early work on Ayers and black recruitment anticipated themes developed in today's best scholarship on slavery and African Americans in the Civil War era. As Peter Kolchin has explained, "historians have increasingly seen blacks not as passive objects of white action but as subjects helping to make their own history." Not only do contemporary historians emphasize "black agency," but they examine minutely "slavery's disintegration under the relentless pressure of changed wartime conditions."[6] Most of all, *The Diary of James T. Ayers, Civil War Recruiter* records the remarkable insight, doggedness, and zeal of an aging midwestern antislavery preacher who was willing to give "everything I have . . . and more had I more, for my Country."

6. Kolchin, "Slavery and Freedom in the Civil War South," in *Writing the Civil War: The Quest to Understand*, eds. James M. McPherson and William J. Cooper, Jr. (Columbia: University of South Carolina Press, 1998), 242, 245.

INTRODUCTION

James T. Ayers was born in Germantown, Bracken County, Kentucky, on November 14, 1805. At an early age he moved with his family to Madison County, Ohio. In 1825 he married Rebecca Bloomer of Fayette County, Ohio, and began preaching in the Methodist Episcopal church. Ayers never devoted his time exclusively to the ministry but he maintained a keen interest in church affairs until his death. In 1831 he joined the great migration of people moving westward. With his young wife he traveled to Illinois and settled first in Tazewell County. Later he moved to McLean County where he purchased a farm near Lexington and reared eleven children. He also owned town lots at Fairbury, in Livingston County. Little is known of his own education except that a later reference to him states that he possessed "fine talents, was fairly educated and a natural orator."[1] His own diary, as the reader will note, indicates that Ayers was not highly trained in formal subjects.

The Illinois to which Ayers brought his family in 1831 was a frontier state eager to expel the Indians. The mention of a certain chieftain named Black Hawk roiled the dispositions of homesteaders throughout the settled areas. People believed that the only good Indians were dead Indians. The enslavement of black men also caused bitter arguments. Many of the original settlers were of Southern stock. Since the completion of the Erie Canal in 1825, New Englanders and New York residents had come west in large numbers. Opinion on slavery, therefore, varied from the aggressive abolitionism of Elijah Lovejoy to a persistent support of the institution recommended by John Reynolds, the Governor of Illinois.

---

[1] *Portrait and Biographical Album of McLean County, Illinois* (Chicago, 1887), 295.

No doubt a large segment of the population was primarily interested in establishing new homes, but slavery agitation was growing from year to year and few men could stand apart from the turmoil. If James T. Ayers ever had any sympathy for the peculiar institution he seems to have lost it soon after he left Kentucky. Certainly his attitude in Illinois was similar to the antislavery sentiment common in Ohio, his wife's state. Ayers' church affiliations may have been the source of much of his antagonism toward the South and Southerners. The Methodist church had a tremendous membership in Ohio, Indiana, and Illinois. Some other sects tried to ignore the slavery issue, compromise the confusing dispute, half- or whole-heartedly support one side or the other, but the Methodists in their 1844 conference decided that slavery was a moral issue. Principles of right and wrong could not be compromised by a sincere ministry and the entire church split into two bitterly hostile organizations.

In Illinois, Peter Cartwright was at the height of his popularity both as an evangelical preacher and as a political representative of the people. He was outspoken in his opposition to slavery. In Tazewell County, where Ayers first settled, many of the people believed in abolition. As early as 1841 an antislavery society had been organized there.[2] It is not surprising that Ayers, surrounded on every hand with sentiment opposed to slavery, joined the militant forces. A feeling of civic responsibility, a desire to serve his community, and his deep religious beliefs, all conspired toward that end. In this period, too, he lost his first wife whom he had loved dearly. In 1858, he married a widow named Mary J. Watson.

The Civil War, when it came, provided an opportunity to crusade against the abuses of slavery. Ayers found himself too old to join the Army. For over a year he watched younger

---

[2] Norman D. Harris, *History of Negro Servitude in Illinois, and of the Slavery Agitation in that State, 1719-1864* (Chicago, 1904), 233.

men enlist and march away to crush people whom he believed to be traitors. Finally on September 8, 1862, Ayers went to an adjoining county and enlisted, giving his age as fifty although he was approaching his fifty-seventh birthday. Elderly Private Ayers was assigned to Company E of the 129th Illinois Infantry and shipped to Tennessee.

At Nashville, Ayers found himself in a Southern state occupied by Northern soldiers. Everyone suffered from the uncertainties of political and economic upheaval and also from rumors of constant enemy forays. Private Ayers was not assigned to recruiting duty at once. The policy of enlisting Negroes for military service had perplexed the administration for some time. At the outbreak of the war in 1861, Northern Negroes had offered to enlist to help free their enslaved brothers in the South. Many of them, like Frederick Douglass, "saw in this war the end of slavery," and their "interest in the success of the North was largely due to this belief."

Many Northern Negroes offered to enlist but both President Lincoln and the Secretary of War opposed using them as soldiers. The War Department even instructed officers in the field to refrain from taking slaves as contraband of war.[3] In the spring of 1862 some Union officers attempted to change this policy. In May, General David Hunter in Port Royal, South Carolina, offered to enlist Negroes in his Army. Soon the 1st South Carolina Volunteer Regiment was organized—but not filled. This action brought considerable criticism but General Hunter maintained that he had not acted beyond authority given him by the Secretary of War.[4] Lincoln, however, was not yet ready to sanction Negro enlistments and he did not relax his policy until the fall of 1862.

---

[3] The reasons which prompted the President and his assistants to pursue this course of action are too well known to require recounting here. For an extensive discussion see Fred A. Shannon, *The Organization and Administration of the Union Army, 1861-1865* (Cleveland, 1928), and George W. Williams, *A History of the Negro Troops in the War of the Rebellion, 1861-1865* (New York, 1888).

[4] Williams, *History of the Negro Troops*, 90ff.

With the issuance of the first Emancipation Proclamation in September, Lincoln began to condone the acceptance of Negro soldiers in the Union Army. A reorganization of Hunter's regiment began in October and on November 7, 1862, the first company was mustered. Meanwhile, other regiments of Negro soldiers were organized in both North and South. Finally, in December, 1862, General Augustus L. Chetlain was put in charge of Negro volunteering in Tennessee.[5]

When the Emancipation Proclamation became effective on January 1, 1863, the federal government accelerated its policy of receiving slaves into the lines and recruiting them for military service. On May 22, a special bureau was established in the Adjutant General's office for the "conduct of all matters referring to the organization of negro troops."[6] General Order No. 143 established a detail of clerks and appointed a competent officer at the head of the bureau. Field officers were detailed to inspect recruiting at various stations. Boards were authorized to examine applicants for commissions to command colored troops. The order stated:

No persons shall be allowed to recruit for colored troops except specially authorized by the War Department; and no such authority will be given to persons who have not been examined and passed by a board; nor will such authority be given to any one person to raise more than one regiment.

The reports of boards were to specify the grade of commission for each candidate. Recruiting stations and depots were to be established by the Adjutant General.[7] Order No. 144, issued on the same day, outlined rules for the guidance of boards examining applicants for commissions in regiments of colored troops. Prospective officers were required to be

---

[5] Fred A. Shannon, "The Federal Government and the Negro Soldier, 1861-1865," *The Journal of Negro History*, Vol. XI, No. 4 (Oct., 1926), 574.

[6] *Ibid.*, 575.

[7] *War of the Rebellion: A Compilation of the Official Records of the Union and Confederate Armies* (Washington, 1899), III ser., III: 215, hereinafter cited as *Official Records*.

physically, mentally, and morally fit. The decisions and recommendations of the board were to be final and any applicant who was rejected was not to be re-examined.[8]

In October, 1863, the program of recruiting Negro soldiers was expanded by the establishment of recruiting stations in Maryland, Tennessee, and Missouri. By this time the government could act with less regard for proslavery allies in the border states, since the danger of secession had passed. Orders for Negro recruiting provided that all able-bodied Negroes were eligible for military service. When loyal owners consented to the enlistment of their slaves the owners were to receive $300 per man. The orders provided further that under certain circumstances slaves owned by masters loyal to the Union might enlist without their masters' consent.[9] A recruiting office was opened in Nashville, Tennessee, with George L. Stearns of Medford, Massachusetts, serving as "Commissioner for the organization of U. S. Colored Troops" with the rank of major. Stearns was an abolitionist who had fought with John Brown in Kansas. When he learned that Negro recruits were being used for fatigue duty rather than combat he protested, but Governor Johnson was sensitive to the feelings of loyal white people in Tennessee. He would not allow the Negro companies to serve in combat. The Secretary of War sustained him in this, and Major Stearns resigned.[10]

To fill his place Captain R. D. Mussey was placed in command. On February 6, 1864, Brigadier General Augustus L. Chetlain was given the command of all colored troops in Tennessee, with headquarters in Memphis.[11] Three days later, Captain Mussey was assigned to the task of organizing Negro troops in middle and eastern Tennessee with headquarters in Nashville. To this station James T. Ayers was sent on de-

---

[8] *Official Records*, III ser., III: 216.
[9] Williams, *History of Negro Troops*, 115; *Official Records*, III ser., III: 1178-79.
[10] Williams, *History of Negro Troops*, 120ff.; *Official Records*, III ser., IV: 90.
[11] Williams, *History of Negro Troops*, 125.

tached service. He had already worked as a recruiter, in the summer of 1863, under Governor Johnson's experimental plan. In Gallatin, Tennessee, in July, Ayers had recruited more than 200 men, and he now felt confident that success would crown his new assignment.

On Christmas Day, 1863, Ayers received his appointment for this special work. He was sent to Stevenson, Alabama, to work under the direction of Captain William F. Wheeler. Upon his arrival there he made the opening entry in his diary. Along the Tennessee Valley in northern Alabama he sought recruits around Bridgeport, Triana, Decatur, Huntsville, and Stevenson. These towns were on the main line of the railroad connecting Memphis and Nashville with Chattanooga. As stations on the supply line to the Army around Chattanooga they were of unusual importance. The Confederates realized this and subjected these towns and the railroad to constant minor attacks, making peaceful life uncertain at all times.

Ayers entered his new work with the zeal which he had shown as a local preacher and antislavery advocate back in Illinois. One of 237 similar agents, his methods are presumably typical of those used by other recruiters. In each town Ayers would nail up attractive posters, one of which is reproduced between pages 28 and 29. These placards announced mass meetings where he would speak to the assembled Negroes and urge them to join the Army. At these assemblies, he gave the Negroes two reasons for enlisting. One was the moral obligation to fight slavery and extend the blessings of freedom to their unfortunate brothers. The other enticement which Ayers offered was the munificent salary of $10 per month, together with free issues of food and clothing.

In rural areas where the slaves remained on plantations, this method could not be used, and Ayers was compelled to ride from farm to farm. He often found the workers in the fields and brought to them, for the first time, news that they were free. Almost always he met stern resistance from white people in the neighborhood. They branded him as a radical inciter of trouble, one who would take security and happiness away from the slaves themselves. Ayers was not affected by arguments of this nature, but he did not achieve the success which he had anticipated. His diary shows that at times he was at a loss to understand why his efforts proved so fruitless.

Ayers' dissatisfaction seems to have been warranted, for the Secretary of War also noticed that the recruiting was not as successful as he had expected. On February 5, 1864, he wired the Adjutant General, then in Nashville, and made inquiries concerning its progress. In part he said:

> I wish you would send me by telegraph a statement of the whole number of colored troops organized, so far as you have information. Some clamor is being raised at the lack of energy and industry on that subject.

General Lorenzo Thomas dispatched the following reply:

> The whole number of colored troops organized and mustered into service in Middle and East Tennessee will number 7,500. In addition, General Dodge at Pulaski has a third regiment nearly full. I now intend to enlist the able-bodied negroes in the employ of local citizens. The people of Tennessee appreciate the views of the Administration, and beyond doubt the recruiting of colored troops in this section will prove eminently successful.[12]

The slowness of recruiting in the spring of 1864 in Tennessee and Alabama was partly the fault of the generals in charge of the occupying armies. In some cases the Army officers feared that the enlistment of Negroes would deprive them of civilian labor necessary in their encampments. Sherman tried to prevent Negro enlistment by issuing an order which in part read as follows:

> Recruiting officers will not enlist as soldiers any negroes who are profitably employed by any of the army departments, and any officer

---

[12] *Official Records*, III ser., IV: 79, 85-86. Perhaps this communication from Edwin M. Stanton prompted General Thomas to appoint General Chetlain to recruit in west Tennessee and Captain Mussey in middle and east Tennessee.

having a negro employed in useful labor on account of the Government will refuse to release him from his employment by virtue of a supposed enlistment as a soldier.

Commanding officers of the military posts will arrest and, if need be, imprison any recruiting officer who, to make up companies of negro soldiers, interferes with the necessary gangs of hired negroes in the employment of the quartermasters or commissary or other department of the government without the full consent of the officers having them in charge.[13]

This order by General Sherman disturbed Adjutant General Lorenzo Thomas, who sent the following communication to the Secretary of War:

I have just been shown the inclosed order of Major-General Sherman, which . . . I conceive will stop enlistments from the colored men coming into his army. I consider the threat of imprisonment to recruiting officers especially harsh. Far better to enlist the negroes, and let them perform their fair share of labor and fatigue duty, than keep them at hard labor—in many instances greater than they were subjected to by their former owners.[14]

An exchange of letters between Sherman and Thomas followed. Then the former rescinded his order. This apparently cleared up the case, but Sherman's counter-order of June 26, 1864, seems not to have reached subordinate officers promptly. In September, Ayers recorded in his diary that he had been arrested on charges of kidnaping Negroes and was sent under guard to Huntsville by order of General Gordon Granger. There he was released by producing his own papers and showing a letter from Colonel R. D. Mussey, out of whose office he was recruiting.

Generals in the field were annoyed by the haphazard manner of enlistments. The organization was uneconomical from the beginning. New contingents were organized before old regiments were filled. Major General George H. Thomas wrote to the Adjutant General on August 9, 1864, as follows:

---

[13] *Official Records*, III ser., IV: 434.
[14] *Ibid.*, 433-34.

I would respectfully call your attention to the following facts and suggestions relative to the U. S. colored infantry service and the plan adopted and pursued by Col. R. D. Mussey superintendent of the organization of colored troops. . . . that of the formation of new regiments exclusively, to the neglect and prohibition of securing recruits for regiments already in existence, and which have not reached the maximum of their organization.

By the formation of new regiments the army is called upon to furnish officers necessary to the efficiency of such organization, and thereby unnecessarily depriving commands already in the field of their officers, or else taking from the ranks men whose services can illy be spared, whereas by the filling up of those regiments already in existence and fully officered this drain upon the army would be removed.[15]

This indictment seems to have corrected the situation to some extent and it is possible that Colonel Mussey altered his original policy.

On October 10, 1864, Colonel Mussey, in his report to Major C. W. Foster, chief of the Colored Bureau in the Adjutant General's office, stated that he believed it inadvisable to organize new Negro regiments until those already begun had been filled. He then outlined a plan for the reorganization of the recruiting program under his jurisdiction. He recommended that all colored recruits be placed under the control of one person. "As it is," he said, "there are regiments formed from the old regiments of whose whereabouts, its operations and success I know nothing." Colonel Mussey proposed that all recruits be sent to Nashville "for examination, enlistment and some drill before they were sent to the commandant for which they are enlisted." A significant statement in the Colonel's proposal was a suggestion that Negroes themselves be used to assist in recruiting. He said:

To make recruiting successful here an armed force of one regiment or more is necessary. . . . Wherever we have been able to send a force of, say, 80 or 100 men for a few days into the country, we have always got men, and the good conduct of the men upon such scouts has left a favorable impression on the people.[16]

---

[15] *Official Records*, III ser., IV: 595-96.
[16] *Ibid.*, 770.

Finally, Colonel Mussey recommended that all recruits be given assurance that their families would not suffer or be persecuted by Confederate sympathizers during their absence.

At the time this report was written, Ayers had resigned as a recruiter, but had previously used some of the methods Colonel Mussey recommended. On July 26, 1864, as Ayers' diary discloses, ten armed Negroes from Nashville had arrived at Huntsville to assist with his recruiting. On other days, Ayers' entries indicate that the promise of security for recruits' families had a salutary effect on enlistments. Ayers did all that he could to assure the families of recruits that they would be protected by the Union Army if their men enlisted to fight.

In reviewing the recruiting of Negro soldiers in northern Alabama, Ayers' area of operation, Colonel Mussey described it as eminently successful. He said that "some 300 were obtained for the 17th U.S. Colored Infantry" and that frequently slaves ran away from their owners to enlist.[17]

To Ayers, however, the progress of his recruiting was not satisfactory, and early in October he went to Nashville and resigned. Several things seem to have prompted him to take this step. In the first place, his zeal would brook no half measures. He had encountered, to his surprise, many Negroes who were not interested in fighting for freedom. Moreover, Ayers was not in a position to see the results of recruiting in the entire area. He concluded that it was a failure and not worth his time. Then, too, by the early autumn of 1864, the time had come for the re-election of Abraham Lincoln. This interested Ayers more than anything else. He devoted his spare moments to writing campaign poetry and songs. He recorded in his diary that Lincoln's defeat would be a national calamity. The state of Ayers' health also discouraged him, and he frequently complained of illness. He felt that ranging around looking for "nigger recruits" who were disinterested

---

[17] *Official Records*, III ser., IV: 768.

was too strenuous for a man of fifty-nine. He longed to return to his regiment and carry on his religious campfire meetings with the men he knew and understood.

In spite of Ayers' discouragement, Negro recruiting in his territory was unquestionably a success, for, of the 186,017 Negroes who served in the Union Army, 104,387 were recruited in Confederate states. Tennessee, the area where Ayers worked, furnished 20,133 troops. Alabama, with only the northern tier of counties in federal hands, provided 4,969.[18]

In the final victory of Northern arms, due credit should be given to the Negro soldier and also to his white recruiter. Definite figures are not available, but the number of colored troops in the Northern Army has been estimated at from six to eighteen percent. Whatever the true figure may be, the Negroes made an honorable record. As recruits they were more accustomed to obedience than the white man. If some of them lacked individual intiative, they made up for it with deadly courage. Fully aware that the enemy had issued orders to show them no mercy, Negro soldiers fought with desperation.[19]

In the fall of 1864 Ayers went north on furlough to vote for Lincoln and Johnson. At the end of his visit he returned to the 129th Regiment. During his absence, this organization had moved with Sherman's Army in its triumphant march through Georgia. Ayers reported for duty at Nashville, but his regiment had already left. He was returned to it by a circuitous route by rail and ship via New York, then down to Savannah, Georgia. Here he found his old comrades and

---

[18] *Official Records*, III ser., V: 662. Walter L. Fleming in his *Civil War and Reconstruction in Alabama* (New York, 1905), 88, claims that many Negroes who enlisted in northern Alabama were credited to northern states. Instead of the official figure of 4,969, he claims that a conservative estimate of the Negroes who enlisted from Alabama would be near 10,000. By order of the provost marshal, General James B. Fry, the recruiting of Negroes was stopped on April 29, 1865. *Official Records*, III ser., IV: 1282.

[19] Shannon, *Organization of the Union Army*, II:162-63. Williams, *History of Negro Troops*, contains many examples of the Negroes' gallantry during the war.

with them reveled in the ruthless destruction which Sherman's Army had perfected. He also enjoyed conducting religious services nightly. His health, however, continued to decline. Private Ayers was finally placed with convalescents where he received some special consideration in the quality of his food and transportation. He moved through Virginia to Washington, where he was "on detached duty, with a view to promotion in the U. S. Colored Troops."[20]

The military career of James Ayers did not terminate with the Civil War. He had learned to like Army life. Furthermore, he was intensely interested in the Negro's future welfare. Ayers felt that he could assist in the difficult task of adjusting these people to their new freedom. Before he was mustered out of his old regiment, he enlisted, on June 5, as chaplain with the 104th Regiment of the United States Colored Troops, was assigned to Company G and ordered to report at Fort Duane at Beaufort, South Carolina, on July 1, 1865. Ayers received his commission as a first lieutenant. Thus he became a wearer of shoulder straps, one of the class of officers whom he had roundly castigated in his diary when recruiting Negroes. James T. Ayers ranked fifth on the roster of officers in the regiment, with only a colonel, a lieutenant colonel, a major, and a surgeon above him.[21]

Ayers' ill health prevented him from giving much service to the 104th Regiment. During the summer of 1865 he was committed to the hospital at Beaufort, South Carolina, where he died of typhus on September 10, 1865.[22] His family was not immediately informed of his passing. As late as November 30, 1865, Joseph B. Ayers wrote to officers in Washington inquiring about the whereabouts of his father.[23] The Adjutant

---

[20] *Report of the Adjutant General of the State of Illinois* (Springfield, 1900), VI:542.

[21] MS in the War Department, Adjutant General's Office, Washington, D.C., dated July 29, 1865.

[22] From the Pension Files of Civil War veterans, No. W. O. 165,560 in the National Archives.

[23] Letters Received, 1865, U.S. Colored Troops, Recruiting, Adjutant General's Office, p. 334.

General was negligent in replying. On January 13, 1866, he sent the following message:

I have the honor to inform you [h]is name is not borne on the records of that regiment [*104th U. S. Colored Troops*] and that his name does not appear on the Record of Officers of U. S. Colored Troops on file in this office.[24]

In all probability the records of the 104th United States Colored Troops were in transit to Washington when Joseph B. Ayers wrote his inquiry. The date on which he received the news is not known. It may be presumed that the Adjutant General's office notified the family when the official memorandum arrived. However, Ayers' service record was never completely filled. Perhaps the hasty departure of the 129th Illinois Regiment and Ayers' enlistment in the 104th United States Colored Troops made this impossible. In any event the only record of his death appears in a published list of deaths and interments at Beaufort.[25] This is perhaps the reason why a request for a pension was denied Ayers' widow in 1868.[26] However, it may be pertinent to note that Ayers who was devoted to his children and his first wife, never mentioned in his diary his marriage to Mrs. Mary J. Watson in 1858.

James T. Ayers was an impressive-looking man, almost six feet in height. He weighed 170 pounds. When he enlisted in the Army in 1862 his hair was already gray. This must have made him unique among the other privates of Company E of the 129th Infantry. Ayers' cheerful disposition and his great faith in his fellow men seem to have made him extremely popular among his friends.

His diary was written in a ledger, eleven and three-fourths by seven and one-half inches. He seems to have used it at first to record loans to his friends and memoranda about petty ex-

[24] Letter Book, Vol. I, U.S. Colored Troops, p. 314, Adjutant General's Office.
[25] Surgeon General's Office, Record and Pension Division, Oct. 28, 1868.
[26] See the pension files of Civil War veterans, No. W.O. 165,560 in the National Archives. A copy of the license for this second marriage is in this file.

penses. Later it became a scrapbook in which he pasted various clippings from newspapers. Finally he apparently decided to use the blank pages for a diary. Thus he was obliged constantly to skip over extraneous entries that he had made previously. In editing this work the daily entries have been printed in sequence. The extraneous material may be found in the appendixes. Poetry which Ayers obviously composed himself is printed in this volume at the exact place where it appears in the diary.

James T. Ayers wrote with fluency and with little respect for conventional spelling. He punctuated his sentences in an original manner and used capitals at will—often in the middle of sentences and seldom at the beginning. A few of these peculiarities have been corrected in order to make the manuscript more legible. Periods have been inserted at the ends of sentences and deleted from places where the author may have intended them for commas. The beginning words of sentences have been capitalized. Moreover, several pages of direct discourse have been recast into paragraphs and enclosed with quotation marks. Otherwise the diary has been printed as Ayers wrote it.

The manuscript has an interesting history. During the last days of the Civil War, James T. Ayers became acquainted with Charles Lawton, a slave who had gone to war as the valet of his master. Once when Ayers moved on short notice—he left his diary and other personal effects in Lawton's possession. Ayers never returned; and the diary became a part of the Civil War mementos of the Lawton family. I am indebted to Mrs. Ogaretta Robinson, a niece of Mr. Lawton, and to her nephew, Mr. William Robinson, for presenting the diary to the library of St. Augustine's College, Raleigh, North Carolina. Miss Pearl Snodgrass, the Librarian at St. Augustine's, brought the manuscript to my attention and stimulated my interest in it. I am grateful to her for this and other manifestations of a deep interest in historical scholarship.

Many persons cooperated in numerous ways in my efforts to edit the diary. Among them were Miss Maud H. Graham, Chief of the War Records Section of the Adjutant General's Department of the State of Illinois; Dr. A. M. Pennewell, Historian of the Rock River Methodist Conference, Chicago, Illinois; Dr. C. H. Thrall, Secretary of the Illinois Conference of Methodist Churches; Miss Barbara Ann Bruntlett, Acting Librarian of Illinois Wesleyan University, Bloomington, Illinois; Miss Mable Brown, Librarian of the McLean County Historical Society, Bloomington, Illinois; Mr. Dan Lacy, Assistant Archivist, Mr. Thomas M. Owen, Jr., Chief of the Division of Veterans' Records, and other members of the staff of the National Archives; Colonel A. Gibson, Librarian of the Army War College, Washington, D. C.; the Adjutant General's Office, Washington, D. C.; Dr. C. C. Crittenden of the North Carolina Historical Commission; Dr. William Clement Eaton, Professor of History, University of Kentucky; Dr. Charles S. Sydnor, Professor of History, Duke University, Durham, North Carolina; the members of the staff of the Duke University Library; Miss Parepa R. Watson, Librarian of the North Carolina College at Durham; and Mr. Jay Monaghan, Dr. Charles M. Knapp, Mr. S. A. Wetherbee, and Miss Mary Lynd Luers, of the Illinois State Historical Library. I am deeply indebted to all these persons for their unselfish cooperation. My wife also helped in many ways, and I shall be ever grateful to her.

JOHN HOPE FRANKLIN.

THE DIARY OF JAMES T. AYERS

A SHORT JOURNAL AND DIGEST
OF TRAVELS

R ECVD my Apointment friday Dec. 25th, 63 at Nashville. Received orders Saturday Evening to Report Amediately to Wm F Wheler General Agent[1] for Col. Recruits at Stevenson Allabamma.

Dec. 28th Report At Stevenson[2] to Capt. Wheeler Ready for duty.

Tuesday Dec. 29 fine pleasant day. Capt. Wheeler not Present. I am waiting his Arival. Stephenson is A small place surrounded with hills and Rocks. Nothing inviting in its Appearance for A Town tho seems to be A good Shipping Point there is at this time A Large Amount of Government Stores and property here and several Reg. of soaldiers and mud no end to it from kneedeep Downward. I have Jus made the Acquaintance of Capt. George W Jones. I am now Rooming with him Nephphew of George Parks of Bloomington seems to be A fine Companionable man better be born Lucky than Ritch so says the oald Adage, so I am fortunate in this Acquaintance of Capt. Joneses I hope. This now in After-

---

[1] It has been impossible to identify William F. Wheeler as an Army officer. Most likely he had been serving under appointment from Andrew Johnson, military governor of Tennessee, by whom recruiting of Negroes had been directed since early in 1863.

[2] Stevenson and Bridgeport, both in Alabama, were vital points on Sherman's rail and river communication line to Nashville and the north. At Bridgeport, some 30 miles southwest of Chattanooga, the Nashville and Chattanooga Railroad crossed the Tennessee River via Long Island by two spans, 1232 and 428 feet long respectively. Stevenson, 10 miles west, was the junction point with the Charleston and Memphis Railroad. On that railroad, between Stevenson and Huntsville, 50 miles west, were Scottsboro and Brownsboro. Decatur, 25 miles farther west, on the south bank of the Tennessee, was the junction point with the Alabama Central, which also ran north to Nashville. Stevenson and Huntsville were heavily garrisoned. Ayers' recruiting activities during 1864 were along this military line.

(1)

noon of Tuesday. J.T.Ayers. [*The author habitually signed each day's entry.*]

Dec. 31st 1863 and At Bridgeport Allabamma. Came her yesterday Evening. The Town has steped out if Any there Ever was. I would suppose from number of encampments scattered all Round there must be over fifteen thousand troops here. The Tennessee River passes by this place. This place is not Mountainious but considerable Broken. Rained Last night Cloudy this morning pleasant and Warm. My health still Prety good have been Round some Looking after Nigger Recruits. Am going to make them A speech to Night and beat up for volunteers. Think the chance Rather Dull here, had my Revolver stolen last nit which Leaves me Defenceless. The River is up prety full. Governent is building a Large Boat here. Everything is in A stir here. Eaven the Mules Are stiring into Bones or are nothing but Bones. Tomorrow will Be New years day 1864. God bless the day Bless thy people parden what has past and give wisdom and grace for days to Come. J. T. Ayers.

In the Evening of Date Above I have Just mailed A letter to John Purdam of Illinois. It is Raining and thundering and Looks Like being A stormy night Bad for my Business sure will all write.

It was so rainy to night I could not speak and Laid it over till to morrow evening.

Newyears morning
January 1st A.D. 1864. Am quiet well. It turned coald as Greenland in after part of night and is verry coald this morning. I am in A tent all alone. good fire and good bunk.

in afternoon of Jan 1st 64
The day has been clear and coald freezing all day. been to the River and to Quartermasters Establishment and to Col

Mcdugals headquarters. Saw the Col and Laid my case before
him   nothing done yet.   Learned from the Col. that several
Soldiers that had been discharged frose to death Last night
here

2nd Jan. 1864 in the forenoon.   Last night verry coald
frose hard   this morning Cloudy and coald bids fair for
storm   no niggers enlisted yet   two cold for niggers
here.

Jan 2nd 8 o'clock at night all alone at Bridgeport. Just hur-
anged a patch of Darkies. got no Recruits as yet. still Cloudy.
not quiet as coald as Last night.

3rd sunday morning Cloudy and coald.   Sent A Letter today
to my Little girl.

Dec [*January ?*] 4th went back to Stevenson

And 5, Leave for Huntsville Ala.   Cloudy this morn and
coald.   All well

Jan. 7th Wednesday morn.
    At Scotsborough on Road from Stevenson to Huntsville.
Staid here Last night.   There is one brigade of soaldiers here
and part of Brigade at Bellfont. Cloudy this morning and
still coald.   Staid with Parson Wood.   Leave today for Huntsville Ala.

Jan. 7th 64.   Landed at Eleven O'clock today at Huntsville
Ala walked from Brownsburg 12 miles to this place. Camped
all night four miles from here at Station house with 5 soaldiers. Oh but it is coald here snowing A Little. Huntsville
is A prety place some four thousand inhabitance here.   Rich
fine Country Round.   I am prety well tired down with my
Big walk tho I am well and am well Pleased here.   J. T. Ayers

8th verry coald Light Sprinkle snow on the ground this morning. Have my quarters in Large Building on south side of square   good fierplace and comfortable   well satisfyed so far. J.T.A.

Do.   I have Just finished A letter for Joseph Ayers[3] of Illinois

Composed by J. T. Ayers on the Loss of his Family[4]

1st, Thare Lyes upon Mount Pleasant hight
The object of my Harts delight
My Loss was her Eternal Gain
She Lived A Christian died the same.

2nd, The plants that grow Around her Tomb
They seem to grow and thrive and bloom
Unconcious that they grow so near
The object of my tender Care.

3rd My two Daughters Ly here two
My Daughters how I mourn for you
I mourn but Still I hope in faith
One day I shall you all imbrace.

4th My Little babe what Shall I say
It had no sins to wash Away
Its gon and Left A world of sin
The blessed saviour took it in.

5 And when my moments are all fled
The Spirit gon the boddy Dead
I hope my friends will then Provide
And Lay me by Companions side.

6 And thare in silence let us be
Till Gabriel Sound the Jubilee
At which Sound we all will Rise
And meet the Saviour in the Skyes.

[3] Joseph B. Ayers was the first son of James T. Ayers. In 1864 he was a farmer living in Danvers, Illinois. He was described as one of the "most progressive and substantial citizens" of McLean County. See the sketch of his life in the *Portrait and Biographical Album of McLean County, Illinois* (Chicago, 1887), 294.
[4] These verses appear in the diary with several others copied by Ayers from current newspapers. The latter are reprinted in the Appendix, pp. 103-33. There is nothing to indicate when or where Ayers composed the above verses.

7th   Oh what A Glorious time twill be
I hope my Children all will see
Will seek the Blessed saviours face
And Heaven and Glory then imbrace.

Huntsville Ala Apr 30th 1864

well it is now Raining slowly and is warm and pleasant 10 Oclock A.—the morning was fine. Rained some in the after part of night. There was one Brigade left here this morning for further front and some heavy artilerry also. I have Just been Round whare those Reg. was Camped, Looking after Darkies for Recruits supposing some would be left behind. And so there was but none seemed willing to inlist. Pore ignorant Devils they would Rather Stay behind and geather up the Boxes, oald shoes and oald shirts and Pants our Boys have left than be soldiers. One fellow I attacted and was pressing him hard to inlist and his wife steped up and said he could not go.

"Why" said I "are you his wife?"

"Yes" said she.

"Well why Cant he go" said I.

"Why" said she "he aint healthy."

"God have mercy" said I "he is so fat and slick his Eyes are all most ready to pop out now   besides he has A mule load on him now. Don't tell me he is sick   and beside you leave. I don't want you. Father Abraham dont want women and haint sent me after them so you may patter.[5] I want your man" said I to her "you ought to be A slave as long as you live and him to if he is so mean as not to help get his Liberty, but sneak Round our camps to live on the Rags we throw away when he might do better." I was A little out of humor you see.

---

[5] To many Negro slaves, Abraham Lincoln was regarded as a Messiah; and merely to mention his name was to inspire respect and obedience among them. *See* Bell Irvin Wiley, *Southern Negroes, 1861-1865* (New Haven, 1938), 15.

Well while Ranging Round I herd for one hour Loud Cannonading and fighting going on down the River below here probably at Decature.[6] I feel verry anxious to hear the news. We are going now from this on to have stiring times. Everything seems to have new life here this morning. Even I myself feel all on Tiptoe. Jas. T. Ayers and still well

Sunday morning May 1st 64. It Rained mostly all night Long but is clearing Away this morn. Troops and waggons were moving all the night and are Still on the move. General Logan[7] and his Command are moving farther front, by way of Decature. Our Citty this morning Looks Rather naked save the moveing Troops passing Along. I understand there is other troops comeing here, probably a part of which will be Black troops. Oh wont Rebs here sware if they have to be garded by sambo. Come Cuffy   gard Massa   make him good. Every Dog must have his day, and it is time De Cuffys should have fair play.   I feel verry much this morning Like I Should Leave here soon. Recruiting has About played out here for the present. J. T. Ayers.

Stille Here this May 2nd 64.
This morning is clear and A little Cool. Looks to me as we should have some setled wether now. From four Oclock up till 8 this morning the Drum and fife has been sounding officers Riding   waggons Roaling   Redgiments marching one after an other. Artillerry two sections was along all of the 16th Army Corpse saturday and yesterday the 15th Army Corpse moved. So all is now on the wing and move front. I am busy now geathering up Darkies. I hope to get A crowd up to day.

---

[6] The skirmish was on the road between Decatur and Huntsville on the morning of April 30, 1864. See the report of James B. McPherson to W. T. Sherman, April 30, 1864. *Official Records*, I ser., XXXII, pt. I: 692.

[7] Major General John A. Logan, former congressman from Illinois, was in temporary command of the forces of Major General J. B. McPherson, who was mortally wounded in July, 1864, during the battle for Atlanta.

May 3rd. Oh how beautiful and Lovely this morning Clear A little Cool, and Everything seems full of life. Even the little forest songsters are tuning there notes to the merry glee. I have just had my breakfast and feel well. Our Streets Look naked this morning. Soalders are prety scierce here now. I feel prety sure that in A few days we shall have stiring news. God bless the write and Crush out the Rong, or Bless the Union and Crush Rebellion. J. T. Ayers.

Speech prepared by J. T. Ayers while at Huntsville Ala May 4th 64.[8]

Ladys and Gentlemen friends and fellow Citizens. I do most Hartily Rejoice this day, and on this occasion, that I am privilieged once more Amidst the Commotions that has been Rendering our Land from Center to Circumference To Appear before you, and I feel greatly flattered today that you have Bestowed upon me so high Honors, as this, to Appear on this platform with my friends. As one of your Speakers, I feel to thank the President and Manageers of this days proceedings for there manifest Partiality towards me, knowing, as I, and they, most Assuredly do and this Audience also, that you have in your midst those more able to Address you than I am, here is my friend———— and here———— and here

---

But for this Partiality Ladys Gentlemen Mr. President and Board, I thank you, yes I thank you with my hart and soul. But now my friends Comes the Dificulty with me, what shall I say to you. How Shall I meet the Common and Rightfully Expected Hopes of this People this day, how Can I or shall I Requite this Respect shown me, in this I fear I shall fail———— Well Ladys and Gentlemen, I suppose you will and do naturly

[8] This draft for a prospective speech, evidently to be delivered before an audience to whom Ayers had long been known, may approximate in theme and content the one he delivered on July 4, 1864, at or near Lexington, Illinois. See p. 40.

Look for some sort of War speech, or A short Historical Account of my Recruiting operations, or A Discription of the Hardchips and fatigues of A soaldiers Life, or A discription of the Common appearance of the Southern States in there present Destroyed—and Shattered Condition, or the Manners and Customs of the People in the South, or perhaps you may Look for something to be said Relative to the Relation of Master and Slave. Wel however much I could say on all those topicks, and however much I would be pleased at A proper time to Speak on all those points, Still it is not my purpose to Speak of those things to day. I could not do them and my self justice here today, without being to tedious and weriing you with A long Harangue which I have no mind to do. It is Enoughf for me and my purpose this day, to say to you my friends, that I have seen A sufficiency since I left my friends, and Home, to assist as best I could in the Defence of our Common Write Gave you and me by God himself through the instrumentality of our Fathers, I mean this most Glorious and best of all other Governments under the Shining Heavens of the Lord, I feel I might speak and perhaps to some extent with interest but time wont now admit———

And with regard to my Adventures and Experiments in the Progress of my Recruiting operations   geathering up Sambo and the many and Conflicting and pleasant as well as unpleasant interviews I have had with Masters and Missuses bout sambo would be pleasing to you more than   Some of it has been to me. For while A part of this Labour of mine has went off pleasantly. Still sometimes it has been attended with great danger and Risk. And many unpleasant things has occurred, I have stood allmost as A lone tree where A forest once was, forsaken by all the South, and while by Brother soaldiers, and officers would occasionally meet a smile from Southern faces, in Shape of Southern Women, My Lot was sneers and Curses. "There goes that oald nigger Recreuter, thats that oald man was at our House the other day, and took pops or dads Niggers Away." And Oh such Eyes and Daggers as I get. Well this is my Comfort. I came not to Court there affections nor to live by there favours, but to serve my Country and assist as best I can to crush out this unholy and Hell deserving Rebellion, and as they waged war on us About the Nigger, why, in Gods name give them niggers, and on this wise, You know the oald Adage is that the Hair of the dog is good for the bite, so they are so Exceedingly tender about there blessed institution and would Rather than be prevented from Raising, and Producing slaves for market as we do Mules and Horses and cattle, they must have our Constitution so attired as that it should be A like lawful to market there Chattles in shape of Human soals, North as well as South, Failing in this now [They] say they will tare down this oald Government And build one Just to our mind, with Slaverry for the Chief Corner stone, and they Lay hold of the Pillers   yes the verry Pillers of this fair fabrick of ours to overturn the whole Superstructure. See they seise our Shiping, they seise our purse Strings, they seise our Harbours our ports, block up our Rivers, and mercilessly fall on a handful of unoffending men, Beseige them with an army of those tigers and Devils, and bumbard   assalt and Maim them for no other Cause, than the Simple fact that they ware the occupants of an American fort, with the Emblem of our Nationality waveing over its Ramparts and over the heads of the American soaldierry thare, and while Surrounded by this gang of Demons in Human form, as Col. Anderson[9] was, famished and in A starving Condition the President sends A Relief party with Bread to feed the Starving soaldier. And those Demons Drive the Angels of mercy Away by fireing on them. Now in Gods

---

[9] Major Robert J. Anderson, who was in command of Fort Sumter in April, 1861.

name what had Col Anderson Done to the South to warant all this. Nay what Had the North done to warant all this. Why, the North forsooth had Elected Mr. Lincon President, and they was Afraid Slaverry would be interupted, not that it was Actually interfered with, but fears were intertained by them it might be. Hence the shedding of blood, the Assalting and slaughtering our Peasable soaldierry dwell here, the seising our finance our Armory our forts, Harbors Navy, and all the Available means of Government with A view of the utter overthrow of this fair fabrick. Surely was enough to arouse any people. Niggers to fight such Demons and Devils,   with Niggers to Cure the bite   Nigger tool to cure Traitorism, Nigger Powder and Lead, seasoned with the Amansipation Proclamation garded and Protected in the hands of A wise and good Administrator, handled by Sambo, at the Britch of A good Musket, Surely is a plaster good enough for traitors, yes or those who are in simphany with them. I mean now Copperheads, yes mean Copperheads, yes Cowardly sneaks, Dirty Slipperry Slimy nasty Copperheads, Pore pukes, the back of my hand to them. Oh say some "You must not arm the Nigger, it will degrade us," Says another   "I would not fight by a nigger." Well I believe that Jake, you have toald one truth sure, you wanted a hobby to Ride on, you did not intend to fight Any how, why sir nine cases out of ten of those mean sneaks wont fight,   no sir I would Rather twice toald, chance the black than the white nigger, and of the two the Black is the best. My motto is, Down with Rebellion, that is my sentiment, and here I offer it. Never cease giving Pills, no matter who ishues the dose, white or black, of Powder and Lead till traitors are subdued And not only subdued, But Efectually so. Why my friends, I would, Could I, make them Available or use them on the field of Battle in the midst of deadly strife, when patriots are Strugling for God and there

Country, Turn Loose in the midst of these most fiendish and
ungodly Traitors, ten thousand times ten thousand Raging
Shrieking madened mules, and Jacks, Tigers, and Even Devils
if Devils would not be asshamed of being Slandered by fighting such unholy Bloodthirsty A set of tirants and usurpers as
those southerners are—yes, I Repeat I am for Any and every
means and measure God and nature has plaiced in our hands
to be vigerously and Earnestly used for the purpose of putting
down this Rebellion and after all is Done and vigerously ap-
plyed, if need be, my friends Lay down my own Life on the
alter of my Country freely, yes freely. Why should I be better
than my Fathers ware, who Laid down there Lives to procure
it for us. Yes they waided throug seas of Blood induring
Poverty   Hunger and thirs[t]   moniless   Barefoot
over frost and Coald   Ragged and destitute and Like
Brave men as they were, bled and suffered to Rear up and Establish for them as well as us there ofspring A pure Republican government Alike free, to and for all mankind. And are
we to crouch and whine and Cower, down to A few Lordly
serfs, and Southern Slave drivers, and in turn be made slaves
of ourselves. Never, Forbid it Lord. They the serfs   we
the mudsills, they the Lords   we the pore white trash, they
the Rulers   we the suppliants. Never   no never   in
Gods name never.

Well as I fered so it is, I have consumed more time here
than I intended, so I pass on to the next thought, that of A Soaldier. Well, I don't here intend to dwell, to fully understand
the Dutys, trials, Dangers, Exposures, and Sacrafises of the
soaldier that is only known by being A soaldier, so, I say my
friends try it for your selves, see that picket boy far in front,
in the face of his Enemy at the Darkest hours of midnight,
with his musket, Trudging his Beat A distance Generally of
forty or fifty yards, backward and forward with death like

stillness. Hear him as I have, sing out "Halt who Comes there," No answer, and boom goes his piece, at the same instant or in quick time, boom goes A half dozen or more, all is Roused   all into Ranks, Line of Battle formed and all harts beating in Anxious thought and filled with uncertainty, how soon the Father Reaches home in such a time as this with A glance of the mind   wife   Children   friends Mother   Father   Sister   Brother. Ah yes and yong mens Loved one. All Loom up before the soldier in this fearful moment of suspence. He hurriedly cansels, Carresses, and hands all over to his God, and in A Low whisper Commits himself to the Great God, the God of battles, and by this time Boom Boom goes the missillies of Death, the ord. by platoons Write and Left Deploy, Double quick march, and Away he goes into the Deadly strife. Tell me Boys if this aint some of the scenes of a soaldiers life. But I must not stop here to dwell, as I do not intend to make A speech on the soaldiers toils tho I would like so to do had I time—but I must get Along.

The Destruction and Ruinous Effects of the war in the south

To fully understand this you will Please go and see. I cannot Describe it to you in such A way as that you would fully understand its Complete Destruction,   farms made Commons, Houses torn down, Burnt dow, Hauled Away for shantys, Towns   Cittys Evacuated   only tenanted by soaldiers, Churches boath in Town Country and Citty Deserted, many of them turned into Hospitals, and then fancy you to be one of those Ruined ones, once A prince, now A beggar, once at home now an Exile and Reb and what all this for ? Have there writes Been assailed by the North ? (Here show what they did enjoy) and when you have strove with fancy and fact, as best you Can, the half has not been thought of or toald, of the utter destruction of the south, the soal Sickens at the sight   Here the south are to blame not the north.

I shall not speak of the manners and Customs today—time forbids. Ill only say it is purely African   dats so, so Ise not guin to say noffin on dat subjecx.   In fact many of the comon and porer classes are more ignorant and Less Cultivated than the Pore Slave. Many dont or Cant Read or write and Dont know County   Town or place, only Dads house, and Uncle Sams Just over yonder. A man to be around as I have been, and indured there ignorance and Stupor, would necessarily feel Proud in once more meeting smiling intelligent faces Like I see today. The Ladys here, God bless them, are not only Able but willing not only to tell us whare they are [but] who they are   where their friends Live   what Countys   Towns   Cittys and Localitys surround them, But are Ever Ready to Lend A listening Ear, and Strongly simpathise with that Lonely yong man, seeking his better part and often given him good advise and Comfortable words. Like Angels of mercy always Ready to do good God bless the Ladys.

I Cant speak of master and Slave till in my next but I must say my Experience is the slaves makes the bread and the Master eats it and spends it in Riotous Living for bad whiskey and soon (here speak of southern vices).

Well I have been for some time telling you my friends what I was not going to speak About to day and now you would like by this time to know what on Earth he is going to say. Well I am Going to tell you some of the Effects of this great Rebellion   Some of its Legitimate fruits. This war Like often times is the case when we take a bad coald, we think oh it is only a bad coald, it will soon be over, but it for want of Proper treatment in time seats itself on the vitals and

Lays fast hold on its victom and if Removed atall must be done with Strong medacines, and strict applyances, and best of care. So in this case "Oh" we said "its but A kind of mad fit   it will ware Away   there will be no fighting, the People of this inlightened Age and Country surely Can settle those Dificultys with out war and blood shead, and if they do fight Oh it wont Last Long." We said it would only be A breakfast spell, we should soon whip the south. The South said, "those Northerners are all Cowardly Scamps, why one southern man Can whip five of those mudsills   those greasy bellyed Hardfisted illiterate green yanks," as they call us all, and boath sides were Ready to deseive and Abuse the publick mind in this way but my friends we soon found And so have they likewise that the Job was A big one. All, yes all north and South found this out. The fuel had Caught on fire, and was not so easy put out as thought for. And hence we have been strugling now over three years and Still the fuel Burns. How many are already slain   how many have died of Disease how many orphant Crys, how many widows tears and wails, how many Bereft Fathers and mothers of there sons, how many sisters and brothers mourn for the Loss of Departed friends, and still the Carnage goes on, and Still will it and must it go on, till this ungodly Rebellion be forever and Effectually Crushed out, and my friends we might Just as soon Look for a sick man to Recover from Disease and be Restored to health, while all the Bile and Elements from which his disease first orriginated are Sprung, still Remaining uncured or un Removed to gain good health and be A sound man, I say we might Just as Rationally look for this, as to hope for Peace or a permanent Cesation of Hostilitys untill the cause of all this is Removed, and thank God that Cause is being Removed pretty freely. God bless the medacine and help the Boil to Come Away. [In] Missourie, Tennessee, western Virginia the medacine has worked wonderful and the patients are some better,[10] and there are strong signs of speedy Recovery. Alabama Arkansas and Mississippi show signs of faint operations. Perhaps with A dose or two more pills they may follow suit, and so it is this Cursed boil and Love of nigger must be purged and phisicked from them, Eare they get Healthy Again. God bless the means and help the Phisic do its office, and that speedily.

And Sorry am I my friends to tell you here this day, that the Effects of this war has been and still is working Ruin and Demoralising and destroying thousands of our young men, middle Aged men and Some of our oald men, officers and privates no Class Excepted, by intemperance and profanity. Men who when at home were sober temperate men, have become Confirmed Drunkards, men who ware Honest men at Home have become thieves and even Robbers, men who were Church members at Home have become Card players and Common swarers and not A few of this class may be found in Every Regiment and when you Approach them if by Chance you can get the opportunity and Speak to them on the subject or attempt to Advise them, "Oh," say these, "men cant be Religious and serve God in the army," and you might as well sing Sams [Psalms] to dead men as talk to them. And this Demoralization is so Contagious and Universal in its Caracter I Tremble for the People when I know, that it is God they are trifleing with lest after he has used us as A people, to Execute his will in the Chastisement of the South, and Looseing the chains of the bondman, he turn in his Righteous indignation and blot us as A people from his foot Stool, after seeing so much of his wrath and indignation pored out on the heads of

---

[10] Missouri did not actually secede from the Union; by 1864 it had ceased to be an important theater of military operations. Tennessee was occupied by Union armies and administered by Andrew Johnson, military governor, in the spring of 1864. The western counties of Virginia had been admitted to the Union in June, 1863, as the state of West Virginia.

those vile southerners one would think men would see, one
would be led to suppose, that after A man had stood and saw
A fellow man Deliberately walk to A certain pit and Deliberately fling himself in whare certain Destruction only awaited
him, that those who stood by and saw the Rash and Destruc-
tive Consequences would hardly venture to do the same Rash
and thoughtless thing, at least for some time afterwards, but
with all the vials of wrath that is being poured out by the
Allmighty on the South for there sins and while God is using
us as instruments in this Great work is it not passing strange
we should be so hardened and desperately wicked, I say
desperately, for our wickedness does Amount to desperation.
Many times for instance I have herd men Hollow
and that to in my own Regiment Hurraw for Hell
who has A dollar to bet. In fact so annoying was several in
my Regiment in this way Hollowing Hurraw for Hell, I complained on them to the Commanders, but that was all. Commanders are but Little better. Why I would Rather Hurraw
for his Satanic Rule Jef Davis at once yes by far, than to be
shouting and Cheering for the Devil.

My friends I say not those things to Reproach the soaldier, far from it. No man can more Reverence and Respect
the Noble Patriotic men who have joperdised there lives and
many thousand shed there blood freely on the field of battle
and there boans now bleaching in A southern Clime to save
this Glorious Country of ours and Defend those time Honored
Stars and Stripes, Ah blessed Emblem, glorious flag thy Stars
and Stripes shall wave when Traitors all ly in ther grave.

The Stars and Stripes shall wave say we
God bless our Cause and makes us free.

Shall I strive to pluck one Laurel from thy brow soaldier boy,
never no never noble boy, I love the, yay my soal loves the,
God knows I Love the union soldier. I only speak in tones of

warning. Beware lest after you have fought and Conquered
our Common Enemy That you fall not by the hand of the great
Enemy of all good the Devil. Again I say be ware   God
help the Soaldier. Be ware, for surely it is A hard place to
live and be truly A christian so many winning ways are those
to call the mind into action, so many wicked influences threw
A round him, that nothing but the sustaining power of God
himself will save us from going Astray, and now in behalf of
the soldier and in Gods name, I call on you yes you here this
day my friends, dont forget the soaldier Boy, bare him up in
your prayers, at A throne of Grace pray for him in Publick, in
private at home in your Closets by your peasable firesides, in
the social Sircle in your familys at every turn and Corner as
you pass Along. We need your prayers, God help you. Pray,
and Heaven bless the soldier, and here I add

> God of mercy grant thy blessing
> Send it down upon us all
> Save us Lord from Rebel bullets
> Save us Lord for this I call
>
> Grant that war and Desolation
> May be banished from our shore
> Down with Traitors gracious master
> Save our Union Ever more.

I offer the following and Close

> The stars and Stripes may they
> Wave Triumphant so long as
> Grass grows green and Watter
> Runs down Stream the beautiful
> Foalds of which may our children
> And our Childrens Children to
> the Lates jeneration be fanned
> by its Glorious foalds.
> The stars and Stripes ever let them be
> The Emblem of our Liberty.[11]

Jas. T. Ayers, May 4th, A. D., 1864

---

[11] Internal evidence suggests that Ayers may have composed the second set of verses, though he does not claim authorship as he does for some others in the diary; he may also, for the same reasons, have composed the verses with which he concluded this outline of a proposed speech. See Introduction, p. xxiv, for the arrangement of verses in Ayers' diary.

I thank you my friends for your kind indulgence and patient waiting. I thank you Ladys that you have Honored me with your presence. The Ladys I hope will not feel that I am Designing to flatter them which would be to them Disgusting, no Ladys by no means do I desire to flatter. But had you, Ladys, as I have been Caged up and, plaiced in the midst of A set of merciless Hard harted sower faced Sharp nosed blue liped Demon Smiled Dagger looks from Eyes and seen as many Hauty Cants and Received as much Haughty treatment as I have from the hands of Human, in female form and then in Gods providence get Back once more to Happy oald America once more as I have, and be Surrounded, As I am here, now with all those Smiling faces and Harty Greetings, you would be anything but Human, if you Could pass the occasion unnoticed and Devoid of feeling.

The Ladys of the Brave oald State of Illinois Ever Ready to bestow there Smiles and best wishes on the weried wounded and famished soaldier. Ever Ready Like Angels of mercy to Administer to his wants and give words of Comfort to the soaldier Boy. The Ladys I say God bless them are, to A man All patriots and soaldiers, Long live the Ladys.

1   The world would be Clean out of fix,
    To take Away the Ladys—
    Jef Davis sure might go to stick,
    No one could fight like Blases.

2   But with the Ladys on our side
    The God of nature for us
    We will free the niggers quell the pride
    And wipe out this Slaverry Curse.

3   Load up your guns My Brave oald Chums
    Well Charge there Ranks once more
    Fort Pillow, Ah the murdered groans
    We will Avenge your [*gore?*]

4 Brave boys as Ever God had made
   Ware by the Traitors hand—
   Shot down Butchered and made to bleed,
   By this Traitorous ungodly gang.

5 Altho for mercy many cried
   And besaught those Demons there
   The Crys of mercy were denyed
   All perished in Dispair.

6 Come my Brave boys Load up your guns
   Gird on your glittering steel,
   And if are we overtake those hounds
   Fort Pillow they shall feel.

7 And altho they for mercy Cry
   Mercy must not be given.
   The murderers death they all must dy,
   Grant it God of Heaven.

8 Show mercy to Rebs such as those
   No my Brave boys No never
   but send them all where bad men goes
   To Dwell in Pain forever.

9 Charge boys Charge, Clean out there Ranks
   Give them your Coald steel
   From Center to Extended flank
   Make them Fort Pillow feel.

                    Jas. T. Ayers, Huntsville, Ala.
                    May 6th, 64—All well.

Huntsville May 6th 64.

Just been to Dinner. Eat harty, had Salit   Aspara-
grass, turnip top greens, good fryed ham   Corn and wheat
bread and buttermilk for Dinner. I am Boarding with or
Rather hiring them to Board me now 2 black women and am
Living fine for A soaldier. My health Never better than now,
but what of all this. Oh I am So loansome way down here.
Soaldiers nearly all gon[12] no one to Associate with, nothing to

---

[12] The troops that had been quartered for months at Huntsville probably had been
withdrawn by Sherman for the campaign against Atlanta, which started May 6, the same
day as Ayers' entry in his diary. Skirmishing between the opposing armies had for several
weeks been active along the Tennessee River below Chattanooga, around Decatur and west
to Florence. Hood was testing the strength of Sherman's lines and attempting, by raids, to
interrupt Sherman's river and rail communications with Memphis.

do but Eat and grow fat, set at my window and watch the
Rebs, as they geather in groups at the Corners to plot Deviltry
and Hatch Secession and for those geatherings Bully Corner
Acrosst the Street North of my office is the most fruitful. They
rally here soon in the morning and a Crowd there mostly all
day. Once and a while I pitch in among them and try to Raise
A dust but they have give me over Long since for A hard Job
boath Men and women. A few days since I came in Contact
with three women. I had just took one of there nigger men
and he had deserted me and Missus had him hid. This hap-
ened in Trianna A Little vilage on the Tennessee River 14
miles from here. I went to Missus house and was searching
for Cuffy and out comes Missus Russeling in Silk and Curls
with two other women, Ladys I suppose they call themselves
and says Missus "What on earth, sir, are you hunting here?
Is Any thing missing?"

"Yes mam my nigger man. Just a few minutes since Run
in at this gate and is missing, and I am hunting for him. Have
you seen him?"

"Why no sir, your nigger man who is he?"

"Why, mam, he is one I just now presst up at the incampment for to make A soaldier of."

"What is his name, Mister," says she.

"Sam he calls himself."

"I dont know anything of him" said she.

"Dont you live here, mam" said I.

"Yes sir" was the Reply.

"Well, mam, not five minutes ago this niger Come in at
that gate, and he cant get out of here only at the same place
without being helped for I have stood in sight of the gate ever
since he entered. He told me he wanted to get his coat and
would come Strait back. I waited but he haint Come." This
Lot was fenced in with Boards Eight or nine foot high nailed

on endwise A kind of nigger Jail or pen with several Houses in and one verry fine House where this woman Stayed. "Well," said I "aint this fellow your nigger?" The niger had toald me his missus Lived there as we Came from incampment.

"Well I gess he is Likely."

"And do you say, mam, you haint seen him within the Last Five minutes?"

"Why dear me I told you once I had not seen him."

"Well now look here, mam, I always want to be kind to Ladys, but you must Excuse me when I tell you you Could not help seeing him and you did see him and have him now hid Away." Thare was A black Boy with me that belonged to the Capt thare he had sent with me. Said I "Joe stand at this gate and watch while I search. I am bound to have this fellow dead or Alive."

Said the oald lady, "what did you say you wanted him for, A soaldier?"

"Yes mam."

"Why he wont make A soaldier" says she.

"Well," said I, "thats my business not yours."

"Well do you not think it is wicket to take our Slaves from us?"

"No mam."

"Why I am A widow woman and have no one else to Chop and hawl wood and see to my affairs but this nigger."

"Why dont you keep [*him*] at home then?"

"Why dear me I do," says she.

"You do, why, Mam, the Colonel out yonder toald me he had been sneaking Round the camps for two months past stealing hard tacks and sow belly, for himself and you, till he was tired of him, and hoped I would take him Away, and now you say you keep him at home. Come tell me whare he is. I am determined to have him."

"Do you take them wether they are willing or not?"

"Not generally, but in cases Like this I do, whare they are Loafing round stealing for themselves and there masters two."

"Well do you think slaverry is wrong?" says she.

"I dont think it is write," said I.

"Well the Bible is full of slaverry."

"Oh yes Mam and so is it full of war and blood shead. Do you think war and bloodshead is write mam?"

"No sir."

"Well I dont think so Either so thare we Agree."

"May I not ask Aint you A minister?"

"Sometimes pass for one, Mam."

"I thought so."

Now up steps Paul pry or who Ever she was and Rather Likely at that had she not been Reb. Say she "and you are A minister then are you?"

"They say so, yes mam."[13]

"Well do you sir feel you are doing write in the sight of God and man to Come here Among us peacible citizens and take our slaves Away? They are our money, beside this one you are after now belongs to this widowed Lady. What on Earth will she do if you take him Away?"

"Send and get her son home out of the Rebel Army. He is there now plotting with others how to Cut the throats of yanks as you Call us." This was A Jolter and choked my Little fair faiced new comer for A while but she Rallyed Again.

"Well if you are a preacher I suppose you believe the bible."

"Well, yes, mam, I profess to, to some extent At least."

"Well, sir, I am prepaired to show you Clearly and plainly that slaverry is A bible doctrine. Why sir from first

---

[13] Ayers had been a local preacher in the Methodist Episcopal church since 1825. *Album of McLean County*, 294-95.

of Genesis to Last of Revelation the Bible is full of slaverry,
and the best of men owned slaves, why Abraham Isaac Jacob
and all the oald fathers and christians owned there slaves."

"Oh, yes mam, we will not fall out here by no means but
Dear woman did you Ever for one Moment Reflect that the
verry same Bible gives A historical Account all Along through
as much or more Even, how men used to have wives. Why
Solomon had three hundred, and not satisfyed with them took
seven hundred concubines. David had several wives and was
still Dissatisfyed, kiled Uriah and took his wife. And now,
siss," says I, "in all good Continence how would you like the
thousand wife sistom Revived? Would you like to be one of
seven hundred Concubines all the darlings of one man or even
the two hundred and 99th Lovely darling who was called wife
of one man or would you be willing some one should kill your
man Just for the sake of putting you Among his herd of wives.
I guess not, you would say give me My Uriah, Ill be satisfyed.
I think it is wrong men should have so many wives. Well
thease are Historical Accounts of former usages and Customs
Among the People which the Bible from some cause keeps
silent only in Davids Case who the Bible says was sorely pun-
ished. And now Ladys I have A good way to go yet this
afternoon. Sorry I haint the time to Discuss this subject longer.
Hope Ill see you again and have more Leisure   will be
pleased to talk with you. You seem like women of inteligence
and are disposed to treat me Courteously for which I thank
you Ladys. I am Aware of the prejudices you southerners
have in favour of the institution of slavery and am prepared
on my part to mak Allowances in that direction."

"Well," said the oald Lady, "I Really like to hear you
talk. You talk Reasonable and Jentlemanly. You must call
Again."

"Thank you," said I.

"Well now," said this Little bewitching yong Blue Eyed fairskined widow tidy Enough for one to eat, "you will Leave Aunts nigger wont you?" Well I leave you to guess whether I did or know. I made A Low Bow with A promise to call Again hoped, they might enjoy happyer days when this war was over and so I left fully intending if ever convenient to Call Again and see them Blue eyes that wore by that little Angel widow. When I had Rode Awhile why said I "that Little woman has Caused me to forget my nigger. Well let him go," so I joged on Humming Away some oald tune to kill time.

And this is only one Case. Those cases for some two months or more ware nearly of every day occurrence and sometimes two or three times A day only the Blue eyed widow seldom do I meet her Eaquals anywhare. She is A Splendid Little Piece of Humanity in Shape of A Female, and gained her Point, and saved the nigger. God bless the Little widow, them Blue Eyes that Little plump Rosy Cheek   them Delicate Lilly white hands that Lady Like Smile   that well Seasoned Christian Like spirit. Man would be A monster Could he Deny such an Angel as this. So my Cannon being Spiked I Rode off, threatening A return at A Convenient season.   Jas. T. Ayers.

> The Recruiting business Let me say,
> it keeps me busy every day,
> A man that cannot learn while he,
> Recruits for Darkies must ignorant be.
> (So think I at least.)

Huntsville Ala May 7th 1864

Lovely beautiful morning. All nature is Laughing and Joyous. The Little songsters are Singing Away. Earth has dresst up in her green mantle   the Little streams are patter pattering and moving onward to the mighty ocean. The sun shines as beautiful as Ever, the moon shows still her dotted

face with the Man and his bundle of sticks standing in her
senter, the Stars are Still briliant and twinkle twinkle Away
Merily as they used to do. All, all seem still in proper Gear
But pore Deluded Sinful man   yes pore Sinful man. All,
all is out of fix, all is Desolation Dark and drearry. What
monsters and thursters after blood we are. What is there man
wont do. Well he wont do write But Loves the wrong because his deeds are Eavil. Oh how nice and Comfortably
might this Develish Rebellion and southern Revolt have been
setled had me[n] wished to do write had me[n] been Disposed to do as they would be done by, or as the Saviour Cotes
it, "as ye would that men should do to you, do ye even so to
them for this is the Law and the Prophets." Had our Southern
Brethren heeded this text of the Saviour thare would have
been none of this Cursed war and blood shead now going on
in our midst at this day. And while I now write here comes
the fife and Drum in Advance of A Regiment of Picket gards
for inspection and are now in Coart House yard waiting to
march to Relieve there Brother soaldiers who have been on
Picket the Last twenty four hours. Pore Boys how I pitty you,
far from home and friends wives and little ones. Fathers
mothers Sisters Brothers all, all far Away and here you are
Patting Away to the flam of Drum and the sweet notes of the
fife. Soon you will march off and separate into small squads
and be assigned your twenty four hours duty and those your
Brother soaldiers Relieved now you Commence your Regular
trudge back and fourth on your Beet. Oh how lonely no
setting down no sleeping, no talking or Corisponding with
any but the gard or officer of the day soaldier Boy I pitty you.
But then those Boys all seem Cherful and contented and Recon-
siled to there Lot. They say my Country needs me and I am
willing to forego all this and even more if need be to
save my Country. My life is ready if need be to Lay

on the alter of my Country, all all everything I have my Life with it all and more had I more, for my Country. Who Can for one Moment Doubt the ishue or end of this that sees the Determined will of those soaldiers in the field. And my friends when you Reflect that this is A war for slaverry waged by those ungodly Southern Slave drivers and Slave breeders, to spread there unholy and monstrous sistom of making merchandise of Human soals all over this best of all governments and thereby blot out our fair name as A free people and Destroy our free institutions and make us Alike, all not only stink in the Nostrils of men but of God himself and A proverb and A Hissing to the world who will then be astonished at our zeal in this Defensive war, for Defensive it is. Wether we will or wether we will forebare God wills the freedom of Pore Ham.

And now my friends I'll give you A sketch of one of my adventures Among many others of similar nature. I left Huntsville in the morning to see what I could see and hunt Recruits all Alone. Took the Pulaski Road and followed on ten miles without meeting Anything to suit in my line. Looking off to my write half mile or so I saw A Large Black place in A cornfield. Said I to myself "there is Sambo." So I let off   Laid down the fence   mounted my horse   Rode through Leaving gap down for we never put up gaps or shut gates that would not be militerry. Beside A man dont know how soon he might wish to go out at the same place Again. Well I made up to the Black patch, and sure Enoughf as Expected here was About twenty women and gals and 7 men all geathering corn. Said "Hellow Children   How do you all do geathering Corn   thats the way to do. Whose farm is this?"

"Master Eldridges, sir."
"Is that his house yonder?"

"Yes massa."

"Are you all his slaves?"

"Yes massa."

"Is he good to you?"

"Not mighty good massa."

"Is he A union man or secessionist?"

"Oh Godamighty Master him Cusses de yankys all de time   says day Come here to kill us all and carry us way and sell us all and dat masa Lincum gwiin send us all Clean of."

"Well your master then swares and cusses the yanks teribly does he?"

"Well Massa" says an oald Grayheaded Darky, "massa dont sware, he methodist man."

"Ah indeed he is A methodist is he?" said I.

"Yes massa and Classleader here and casorts some times Oh yes."

About this time one of the niggers said "we must go to work, massa flog us he see us idle and he will ask us who dis man is and he whip us for talking with you."

"Well," said I, "dont be scierd Children I have Come to tell you good news, and I want you all to Listen. Father Abraham has Declared you all free   you have no master now. You are free and I have Come to tell you."

"Bress God," said two or three voices at the same time.[14]

"Well children see here" getting off of my horse then and handing them one of my Recruiting Pictures[15] "here is what Father Abraham is doin for you" showing them the Darky in Center with flagstaff flag waving and on the write, men knocking off the chains from the slaves wrists and some

---

[14] It is significant that seventeen months after the Emanicpation Proclamation, there were Negroes who had heard nothing about it, even in areas that had been occupied by Union forces since January 1, 1863.

[15] See the facsimile of Ayers' recruiting poster opposite p. 28. The original was pasted in the back of the diary.

Just has got Loose and hands stretched upward shouting and Praising God for there Deliverance and on the left side A free school in full Opperation with miriads of Little Darkies Each with his Book, then on other side in Large Letter "All slaves were made free by Abraham Lincoln President of the United States Jan 1st 63. Come then Able boddyed Collered men and fight for the stars and stripes." You would have to be present to understand the Joy of those pore down trodden Abused People. "Well now Children" said I "Father has been good haint he."

"Oh yes bress God."

"Well now he wants you who are able to fall in Ranks and help us A little. We need some help, he offers ten dollars A month and Cloath you and feed you and make you free if you will inlist and be soaldiers.[16] How many of you boys will Turn out?"

"When do you want us Massa?"

"Want you Rite now."

"Oh massa wont let us go."

"Never mind your Master you have none. I'll see to that your master shant hinder you." Well four concluded to go. One said he wanted to go up to the house and get his Coat and see his wife. "Yes of course you all go to the house and get your dinner. I want you all to go with me to Huntsville. Who lives up at yon house Boys?"

"Master Blackwell."

"Has he got any Boys?"

"Yes massa."

"How many?"

"Oh 8 or 10   some oald do [*though*]."

"Well now geather up take your wagon and go up home and get some dinner. Make haist. I go round by that house

---

[16] White soldiers who enlisted in the Union Army were receiving $16 per month by 1864.

RECRUITING POSTER

All SLAVES were made FREEMEN

BY ABRAHAM LINCOLN,

PRESIDENT OF THE UNITED STATES,

JANUARY 1st, 1863.

Come, then, able-bodied COLORED MEN, to the nearest U. S. Camp, and fight for the

STARS AND STRIPES!

THE BACK OF RECRUITING POSTER

and be up at your house directly and if master Comes to you and says anything tell him an oald man Come to you and sent you up and said he would be here soon. Never mind Anything he says. I'll protect you Boys." So Away we all went. Well I might tell some things took place at this place Rather Amusing but I pass. I got two fine big boys here and started write Along, and now for Eldridges. When I got thare all was in Excitement. I Rode up and says "Well how are you all Children of mortality? Hope you are all well." Raised my hat A little. Says to Master, Missus and galls, "How Do you friends, Fine day this."

"Yes" say the oald feller and stepping near me says he "what's all this mean? My niggers say you Come into the field and set them all free, is that so."

"Yes sir."

"Well I would like to know how you got the autherity to do so, Sir."

"By the War Department, sir, I get my Autherity, the verry best of Autherity aint it."

"What do you want with my niggers?" says he.

"Your niggers youve got no niggers my dear sir. These are all free men as you or I am and thease women here that have been your Slaves are all free now as much so as this Lady" turning a little, "your wife I suppose or these yong Ladys your daughters I presume. They are all free, so Declared by the President some time since. I would of thought you knew something About it" turning Again to the Darky women and Children. "Master never toald you you was free did he?" They said nothing. Said I, "No not he Pious man is he keeping men and women here ignorantly in Bondage when he knows they are free as he or his wife or daughters are."

"Well" say the man, "I want you to leave and that soon to."

"Leave, why sir I will when I get Ready. But I am going to take your men or thease men when I go. You may bet your Eyes on that and if you Sower up much at it and show the secesh dog you might get Hurt before you know it;" and here I drew my trusty Revolver out of scabbard. "I shall not hurt A hair of your head, sir, if you be quiet, but I have Come for your Darkeys and your Darkeys I'll have."

Here the oald man turned Away, and his daugter A woman some 20 years of Age, who was married and her husband in the Rebel army which fact I knew, "well" says she, "Mister are you going to take dads niggers Away from him wether they are willing or no?"

"Well no mam I aint, But I'll tell you siss what I am going to do and am in the habit of doing. I find it best to do so. I am going to take all your Black me[n] off half mile or so and have a big talk with them and all I can perswade Away I shall take and such as are two oald and such as I cant coax off may stay. I'll send them Back if any thare are."

"Well," say she, "wont you let dad talk with them first?"

"No mam," said I, "Siss," says I, "do you keep a bible here?"

"Yes sir" says she.

"Well I am going now to tell you of A little sircumstance, you will find in your bible and no doubt have Red many times. It is this, once there was A mighty famin all over the Land and so migtily did it prevail that Boath man and beast suffered greatly. This famin was foretold by an oald man who while the famine continued was sent into the wilderness and Dwelt by side of A little Brook and Ravens fed him. Do you Recollect?"

"Oh yes."

"Well hold, this Little Brook Dried up and then he was sent to A certain place to be Cared for by A widow. So you see he gets him up and Away he goes and what do you think? Why sir, he meets the verry Person who he Expected to feed him geathering or had geathered A bundle of sticks to bake the Last morsel she had for her and her son to eat and then Lay down and dy. Never the Less the oald fellow was hungry and tired and had not Came so far to make A fool of things I suppose he was in Earnest and, said he, never mind I want A little Cake first. Now Siss," says I, "I want my little talk first."

Then she says, "well I no you aint as good A man as that man was."

"I dont know Siss," says I. "You and me wasent there was we."

"Aint you A Preacher" says she.

"A preacher, mam, did you say? Why I have been now more than one hower Preaching as best I know how and thou sayest to me 'aint you a preacher.' If you dont Receive this for Preaching you would not know preachers tho they Should Rise from the dead."

"Well," says siss, "are you a man of A family, sir?"

"Why Siss," says I "would it not be Rather strang indeed if A man Should live to be my age and Love women as well as I do and be possessed of my temperament should not have A family would it not dont you think Sissa?" and I Laughed her full in the eyes.

"Well," says she "you dont answer my question. I thought if you was A man of A family you Surely would have some feeling and not take those men Away from ther familys if they dont want to go. Beside I dont know how Pah is to live, he is now oald and Cant work. And the yanks have taken all our Horses and cattle and grain we have. Why Pah will Starve."

"My dear mam Pah is not as oald as I am no indeed. Let him spit on his hands and Learn to work or you can send if you choose for your Husband, have him Come Home. He Can help pah work and will be in better imployment than whare he is now," says I, "Siss I think your Appeal to me wishing to know if I was A man of A family, Presuming that I in that Case Could not take thease men from there familys I say it grates on my years. How do you folks do? You sell father or mother or Child from mothers brest sometimes sending them far Away, Never to see Each other again and when they have beged you on there knees to not do so you have Driv them from your presence or Lacerated there Backs for having the impudence to ask you such a question, yes indeed. And now all of A sudden you are verry sympathising. Away with such simphany as this."

"Well," says Siss stepping Close up to me and Looking Daggers in my Eyes, "I want to tell you sir I hate you."

"Oh yes sissa" says I, "you do, well I guess you don't pray much here."

"Well," says she "I dont thank you for your instructions nor your impudence. I want you always to know sir I hait you in my verry Hart."

"Oh well," said I, "now I know you dont pray surely not, and now siss I'll tell you as you asked sometime Ago. I have A family   have Daughters oalder than you, think perhaps as much of my Daughters as A father ought to.[17] My Daughters thing oald dad is tolerably Clever."

"Well," says she, "I pitty that woman that would Raise A family by such a man as you."

Well, this stumped me for the moment, for all most involunterily the natural answer was at hand, and I caught myself just in time to prevent the Retort—"A man would [*be*] Awfully pushed to have anything to do with or Raise A family by such A slut as you are." "Well," says I, "Siss I am A

---

soaldier and they sometimes are not verry smooth with the Ladys. Beside I am an oald man, Children nearly oald Enoughf for your Father or mother and beside this I have treated you good humeridly and polite instead of me being the Blaggard you have turned blaggard." Look at it, "A woman must be hard pushed to Raise A family by such A man as you." I had a hard effort to keep myself from turning blaggard two and Retorting but am glad I did not. "Siss, I am Ashamed of you. Your are A disgrace to the sects [sex]. Shame on you Siss."

Here the oald Lady steped up and says, "Anny," taking her by the arm, "you had better go to the house, Child."

"Yes," says I "she had I think so to. Is that your Daughter?" Getting no answer, says I, "if she is I am sorry for you. She is A disgrace to the mother that gave her breath." I then says, "you may as well all go to the house. You will fair just as well for I am determined to have those men."

So they Left and so did I with four of his nigger men and the two I got at the other Place. Those Boys are now in the 15th Tennessee Col. Reg. at Nashville, and I am still here at this cursed Cecesh Citty. Well I keep geathering the Boys in slowly But I want to get Away from here as soon as I Can, so I end here. Health good, spirits fine and all write. Jas. T. Ayers.

Huntsville, May 8th 64,

Sunday morning, Clear, and Just Cool Enoughf to be pleasant and Comfortable. Just had breakfast and feel first Rate. Nothing new in the news. Line Sargent Fields is gon to Nashville with some of my Recruits. Look for him Back this Evening on train. No Letters yet from Illinois. Sent Joe Apr 6th by Express mail fifty dollars and Henry[18] five dollars. Had no word yet from it. J. T. Ayers.

---

[18] Henry C. Ayers was the youngest son of James T. Ayers. He was, at this time, studying medicine in Chicago.

Huntsville Ala. May 10th 1864.

7 o'clock A.M. it is Raining and verry pleasant. We need A little Rain here to Lay the dust which was getting prety bad. There is quiet A stir here this morning; it is Reported that Forest[19] is marching on this place as fast as he can and altho thare has been A Fort for the Defense of the Place in Construction or being Constructed for the Last month Still our Commanders have been so presst with there Arderous dutys of waiting on secesh women, yellow girls, and seeing to there wants subject to the craving of human nature and Riding Roun in Buggys and fine Carriages and Drinking now and then A Little spirits just to keep them Cool and Clear headed that the fort has been neglected and now when in all human probability we shall need and that seriously to [use] this fort it is only Just Commenced. It might just as well have been done as not, no need of this delay. We knew forest was in our Country. We knew he had just butchered Fort Pillow.[20] We knew that without this fort we was Defenceless Just as well two weeks since as we know it now. Why then this delay. Well the women must be seen to and A little whisky drank, and a little pleasure Wriding down if all the me[n] and soaldiers here are butchered this is the way the Land Lays and thease shoulder Straps must be smiled on by the Ladys. Oh yes. I wish to God one half of our officers were knocked in the head by slinging them Against A part of those still Left. We Could do better with the Remainder than with all. We have here now but few men and that few are scatered all

---

19 After the Fort Pillow incident, the mere mention of the name of Nathan Bedford Forrest, the Confederate general, inspired considerable ire among many Union troops. The news of the incident—the so-called "Fort Pillow Massacre"—had spread rapidly, and the alleged atrocities of "butchering" Negro soldiers there had the effect of engendering genuine hatred for him in the Union Army.

20 The massacre at Fort Pillow had taken place on April 12, 1864. Several hundred Negro soldiers were reported to have been killed when the Confederate soldiers refused to permit them to surrender as prisoners of war. For a full account of the incident, see James G. Randall, *The Civil War and Reconstruction* (Boston, 1937), 506-07; Robert S. Henry, *"First with the Most" Forrest* (Indianapolis, 1944), 248-68.

Round in Different Squads. So in Case of an Attact Against
[us] we Posably Could Rally   if Rallay we ever do at all
Forest could have the whole place in ashes and half of us
gobled up. Well we will see what we will see, but as for me
I never will Run nor surrender. I'll dy first. Last Evening there
was A notice Came to the Christian Commission informing
them that At Larkinsville A little Town 35 miles from here
on Rail to Stevenson that there was some 500 or more starving
Pore Refugees who would all perish if not seen to Amediately
    that they had A large portion of them been getting Ra-
tions at the Comissarys but the Brigade now was gon front and
they Could get none. So Chaplin Meril packed up our Traps
and went to depot to take the train Due from Nashville at 8
o'clock P.M. and we waited till ten and no train so we Returned to our quarters and now 10 O'cl. a.M. and no train yet.
I have not herd the Cause of this delay. I think the Late order
by General Shearman will work well. His order is to Ishue no
Rations to no none-Combattants of any Class or Coller only to
soaldiers and soaldiers familys. All others if protected in Any-
way must go further Back in the Rear, that Comisarys must not
Either Ishue or sell nor in Any way either Directly or indi-
rectly feed or aid none-Combitants here in the front. This
will Drive from our midst those who have been in the habit of
getting Rations of us to Live on and at the same time giving
all the aid and carrying all the news they could to our Enemys,
and I hope will help to Drive Away from our midst A Large
Portion of those dirty sluts who are here specially for the Ac-
commodation of shoulder Straps. I think the measure A good
one. "Let the dead burry there dead but follow thou me,"
says the Saviour, and I think it will do here to Cote thus. Let
the Rebs feed the Rebs, and Reb men wait an Reb wome[n]
and Let us follow up our trade of administering powder and
Lead that is the best food we Can give those Devils. If they

Dy let them dy, whose falt but there own.   They brought on
this war not we.   No, let them Rip, is my way, it is good
Enougf for them.   Why sir the Haughty Stinking heiffers
Here in Huntsville will go and Draw there grub of us and
with there mouth filled with our bread treat us with utter
Scorn and Contempt.   Yes sir, thease proud Stinking Heiffers
do this Eevery day.   This I know is so.   Lets Clean them out;
give them Pills Boys instead of Bread, and kicks instead of
huggin and kissing; that is all the way we can manage them
I think.   Have just been To office and Expresst Joe $100 dol-
lars in care of Fred.

J. T. Ayers

Mad but well and wide awake.—May 10, 64.

Saturday morning May 14th 64.

Still here at Huntsville Ala. and well this is one of the
Loveliest morning.   All Around Looks gay and green as tho it
was mid summer.   All faces Look Cherful and harts feel glad
at the good news of our success in the Potomach Army and
Shearmans success.[21]   We feel that Cecession is gasping its Last
now.   (I said all Harts) no not all for those ungodly secesh
men and wome[n] here Looks Like motherless mules and
have there years Loped as bad as you ever saw the years of A
mules daydys year Loped, tho they keep mighty Still, dont
Bray much.   I sent A small lot of nigger Recruits Away yestarday to Nashville by Sargent Field.   We are taring Away at
our Fort now.   It begins to Look somethin like soon being A
place of some security.   We have four guns mounted now and
will mount fore more to day.   So if Forest will just hoald on
A little we shall be in some sort of fix to attend to him in A

---

[21] Ayers had just received word of the dramatic events that had occurred May 5-12 in
the Battle of the Wilderness, where the Union Army of the Potomac was under the command
of Grant.   Probably Grant's staggering losses were not known in Alabama at the time.   It
will be recalled, also, that Sherman had begun his celebrated drive against Atlanta during
the first week in May, 1864.

Saturday morning may 14th 64

...till here at Hughsville Ala and well

...is is one of the Loveliest morning all shower...
...oks gay and green as tho it was mid...
...ummer all faces look cheerful and harts...
...l glad at the good news of our success...
...the Potomack army and Shermons...
...keep we feel that Secession is gasping its...
...st now (I said all traits) no not all for...
...se ungodly secesh men and women here...
...ooks like motherless mules and have...
...ive years Soped as bad as you ever sow the...
...ars of A mule days days year Soped tho they...
... up mighty Still dont Bray much I sent...
...small Lot of nigger Recruits away yesterday...
...Nashville by Sargent Freeling We are...
...ing Away at our Fort now it begins to...
...ook somethin like soon being A place of...
...me security we have four guns mounted...
...ee and will mount four more to day...
...if Forest will Just hoald on A little while...
...hall be in some sort of fix to attend to him...
...A becomeing way our Late changes has...
...the way of Commanders has been for the...
...tter I think how long it may Last I have...
...idea perhaps not Long, as our shoulder...
...raped men are all powerful in hunting after...
...iniline perhaps when they as there predirisory...
...re done before find the proper binioline...
...by two may get so ingaged and interested in...
...t Line as to forget there duty I hope not...
...wever what A pitty it is so many puffed up...
...hoalder Straped fools Act So, man is A strange...
...ing the more favors he has bestowed on...
...him the bigger A fool he is or often So —

becomeing way. Our Late changes here in the way of commanders has been for the better, I think. How Long it may
Last I have no idea. Perhaps not Long, as our shouldered
straped men are all powerful in hunting after Crinoline, perhaps when they as there predisessors have done before find the
proper Crinoline they two may get so ingaged and interested
in that Line as to forget there duty. I hope not however.
What A pitty it is so many puffed up shoulder straped fools
Act so. Man is A strange being   the more favours he has
bestowed on him the biger A fool he is or often so. We have
fine Health here now and all goes off well.   J. T. Ayers.

Well here is Sunday morning and still I am well this
Beautifully fine and Clear [day] and Just Cool Enoughf to be
pleasant. News from Front Gloriously good. Oh who would
not feel fine. God Bless our Land and Nation. God bless
The President His Cabinet Bless Lieut. General Grant, give
Him A Clear head, A Soaldiers Hart, and Victory over our
wiley foe. Send Destruction on Lee, Blot Richmon [Rich-
mond, Va.,] from Record, Down with Rebellion and Restore
Peace once more is my prayer.
    Huntsville Ala, May 15th 64.   J. T. Ayers.
    N.B.   I sent Joseph A Nashville Union [newspaper] this
morning. J. T. A. May 15th.

Huntsville May 19th 64. Just returned Last night from A
trip to Athens in Lime Stone County after a yellow girl. Her
mother hired me. I found the girl six miles from Athens out
in the Country in the field plowing A mule All most naked. I
Brought her Away. While on this trip the Rebs attacted and
bust Madison station, took 60 of our men prisoners and tore
up track so I was Delayed one day at Athens as this was on my
track I had went and had to Return. Prety Exciting times here
now, our weather here is beautiful now, had A fine shower of

Rain night before last. I dont feel verry well today. I suppose after I wrest A little I'll feel better.   J. T. Ayers.

Huntsville Ala May 25th 64[22]

I have Recvd on Deposit of John Anderson Col. man $117 dollars Michigan money Kalamzoo Rail Road Bank to test its value. If worth anything to Account to him if not to Return said Bills to said Anderson who Has now inlisted in the service of the U. S. service in Col. Department. His Wife Lives in or near Huntsville Ala and her name is Maryann Jane Prewett who lives two miles East of Town on the Brownsborrow Road to the Left of Road as you goe East, Large frame House Close by Road side.   Jas. T. Ayers
Rec. Ag. U.S.C. Troops

June 7th 64. Well here I am now this Tuesday in afternoon. Just landed here this forenoon. This place, Clarksville, is on Cumberland River. Contains I am toald some five thousand inhabitance, tho it is Rather an oncitely place. I have Reported to Mr. Morse Recruiting Agent here as ordered. I am inclined to think that this is not the place for me and presume I shant Stay Long here. The wether is quiet warm here now my health is good now. Nothing new now to Record. I Expressed yestarday 6th June $100 to Joseph B. Ayers, have now $45 on hand.   Jas. T. Ayers.

Thursday June 9th

Left Clarkesville with 18 Col. Recruits for Nashville. River quiet Low now only three and 1/2 feet water on Harpeth Shoals. Landed at Nashville, mustered my Boys into two Rank and one of them had A fiddle so we took the streets for Headqrs   fidler in front playing Away. Some big eyes made

---

[22] This item did not appear in this sequence in Ayers' diary, but has been inserted by the editor in its chronological order.

you had better believe. Capt. Mussey is now gon to Louisville,[23] will be back tuesday and then I posably will have A new field of Labour assigned me, I hope at Bowling Green. I have Just been to meeting, herd A tolerably fair sermond, got back to my Board, had dinner and now feel well. Friday in afternoon we had one of the hardest Rains I most ever saw fall. The Streets was completely flooded, but today is beautifully fine.   Jas. T. Ayers

June 16th 1864, At Nashville Tenn.

This is A beautiful day, Just cool Enoughf to be pleasant. Have been up to Capt. Musseys office. The Capt has not yet Returned from Louisville whither he went on last friday. On my way to his office this morning I caled for A while at Post office corner and while sitting there I could but notice among other things two girls appearently 14 or 15 years of Age seated side by side on A small box with Each A basket filld with Lemmons and oranges, and to see there ingenuity in selling to the passers by was to me quiet Amusing.

"Heres good sweet oranges two for ten cents" one would say and the other would sing out "two good Lemons for ten cents," and the boys was buying prety freely.

I thought I would see what those girls names ware and make A little note in my Book, so I stepped up and says, "Well girls you seem to be good salesmen. What is your names?"

The one nearest me gave her name as Ducks Bowen, the other said her name was Mandy Cary Pondy Bondy. And Then the first Girl says, "what do you want to know our names for?"

"Only," says I "to make A little minute in my Book for

---

[23] Reuben D. Mussey, the current director of recruiting in this area, was in Louisville conferring with Adjutant General Lorenzo Thomas on various phases of the recruiting program. General Thomas spent several days in that area consulting agents and others concerning the recruiting of Negro soldiers. *Official Records*, III ser., IV: 433.

my Amusement. I am so pleased to see you such good sales-men."

Says she, "If you ask me my name any more I'll knock you down."

I says, "why siss I mean no harm in the world," so I walked off prety fast at that. Thinks I to myself, "oald man you haint Learnd it quiet all yet. You aint posted in Southern sivilization yet or you would not have the impudence to ask A Little girl what her name might be." I hope those Little girls will Excuse an oald man for be so impudent as to inquire there names. I'll not do so Anymore, nor will I trouble there oranges but must be more modest for time to come and studdy southern sibilization. I am boarding now at Mrs. Ginnings on Cherry street near fire ingine no. five and near News Depot and oister saloon.   Jas. T. Ayers.

[*Shortly after this entry Ayers went to Illinois on fur-lough. The next entry was written after his return.*]

At Nashville, July 13th 64.

Have Just been Home on Leave of Absence. Found my friends all well, had A good time of it in general. Spoke to A Large crowd at Musquietoe Grove, Mclean Co. on saturday near my sons. On the forth we Celebrated at Lexington[24] had About 15 thousand people there. I was Chief Marshall of the day and was calld to the stand and spoke I guess to general Satisfaction. We collected for Christian Commission 23 hun-dred dollars for use of sick and wounded soaldiers[25] Brave

---

[24] This was near the farm of Ayers' son Joseph. The latter "in early life purchased a farm at Mosquito Grove in this county which he occupied for thirty-five years, and where he carried on agriculture with fair success, and his sons now occupy." *Album of McLean County*, 294.

[25] The United States Christian Commission was organized in New York in the fall of 1861 at the suggestion of Vincent Colyer of the Young Men's Christian Association. As a welfare and service organization, it devoted its funds and its energies to the distribution of Bibles, tracts, and hymnbooks, and "offered various forms of diversion to relieve the ennui of camp life, supplied magazines, and sent soldiers' money home to families." See Randall, *Civil War*, 635; Margaret Leech, *Reveille in Washington* (New York, 1941), 217-18; Arthur C. Cole, *Irrepressible Conflict* (New York, 1934), 332-33. Ayers seemed particularly interested in the work of this and similar organizations during his entire time in the Union Army.

Liberal Harts are those Northern People. Can Anyone doubt the ishue of this war while such A spirit of Liberality and Patriotism prevails, Never. Everything is in A flourishing state in Illinois. Corn, wheat, oats, and in fact the farmers never was more prosperous than now and one to travel over the North would scierce know war was in Existence in this once happy Land of ours. But in the midst of my injoyments while on my visit the Sad tidings of the Death of my Lovely Daughter Mrs. Mary Jane Porter and her two Daughters[26] So grieves me. All my happiness for the time was Eclipsed. Oh God how uncertain is Life. What worms we are. We but live today and Dead tomorrow. What A contrast now and A few years gon by, once blessed with A Dear Companion and ten Harty Roasy Cheeked Children, all in the midst of Peace and plenty, Surrounded with friends Everywhere. What Joyful days passt then Along, but A Lass the fell Destroyer Came Along and with his sickle has swept my family Away. There only now Remains myself and four Children her this side the River while My Dear Companion and [word left out] has Crosst over the Stream of time with the other six. I sometimes allmost Envy them, they having been favoured with the first opertunity of Emigrating to that Lovely Country where war and strife sickness sorrow and pain are always A Stranger. Thats A good Country, peace and Joy Reign there. God help me and the four who still Remain to be Ready, that when we are Calld to Emigrate for Eternity we may Be Ready to push off and in the society of that Portion gon on in Advance be Safely Landed in Gods Glorious kingdom. So do I pray and so will I ever pray. The wether here is warm now. I did think of going today down to Huntsville but misst the Cairs, so am still here. No not yet just where I shall go as Col Mussey is Away But Looked for this Evening. When he comes I'll be Stationed soon.

---

[26] See verses by Ayers on p. 4.

July 14th 64 afternoon, sitting in Porch at Mrs. Gennings whare I Board.

It has been verry warm today, have Just been uptown to Headquarters and Reconnoitering Round. Plenty of Country folks Come now to town with Chickens, Eggs, Potatoes, Cabage, Onions, peas, Beans, Apples, Roastin years, Blackberrys, and so on. Boath white and black, it is hard to tell which is the nigger the white or the black. The Dialect is all the Same and So is the manners only the nigger is Rather the Politeest and best Salesman. For instance as I passt on the Street I herd A white woman and A Darkey woman who had been in Each with one horse waggon with marketing.

The nigger woman Drives up and says, "How you Comes on Missus. Sally sol ot yet?"

"Yes," was the answer.

"Why yous got some Apples yet in dat dare Bag dare."

"Oh yes," say Sally. Then Sally says, "Mime have you soald out yourn?"

"Oh yes," says Mime. "Clean done soald Long Ago Every single thing."

At this Mime saw some Rosting years in Sallys waggon. "Oh yes Dare now yous not soal all your Corn. Ise beat you so I has."

"Well you has taken more pains to Run Round and hunt byers than Ise done" was the Reply. The[y] both Laughed just Like niggers. Well its all nig down here, that so. J. T. Ayers.

Wednesday after Dinner, Huntsville Ala July 27th 64.

Yes I have got back here once more to start Afresh Recruiting. Lieut. Hull[27] Came here Last Evening from Nashville with ten Col. men Armed to assist me.[28] The Lieut and

---

[27] Colonel James S. Hull of the 37th Indiana Foot Volunteers was a member of the board to examine officer candidates for colored troops. *Official Records*, III ser., IV: 766-67.

[28] The use of armed men to accompany recruiters was in line with a policy which Colonel Reuben D. Mussey was to adopt generally in October, 1864. In his report he said: "To make

me have been busy all forenoon Getting quarters Camp Equipments Rations and so on and Establishing our Camp and now
for Darkies. We are now going to try for two or three Com-
panys here with understanding that they are to Remain here
as gards to do duty here. We have had Rather A fine little
shower of Rain here this morning and it was greatly needed.
We feel well over the new of Shearmans victory and the Capture of Atlanta,[29] but our Rejoicing is greatly Eclipsed and
mared, with the sad news of the death of our Brave General
Mcferson.[30] All mourn his Loss. J. T. Ayers.

Friday, July 29th 64.

Just returned from A scout of two days Down to White-
burg, had ten Colored troops with me armed. Brought in five
Recruits, had some Jolly times in this trip. I got some 15 men
but some was Lame some Ruptured some pane in back some
Rumatism some toothache and so on till five was all the net
of my trip. I caught 2 deserters but they Boath made there
Escape through the Carelessness of the gards. I find myself
verry tired as I walked all the whole trip and wont do it Again.
The fact is I am pretty tired of this business Anyhow and
Reaally we have Rather two many Cooks here and to many
Commanders Just now, Oh but aint I down in Dixie. What a
cursed place it is I wish [?] out of Dixie, it is verry warm
here now. Had A fine Rain here yesterday.—

Again, Septr. 5th 64

here I am At this Little Stinkhole place, Trianna, on the

---

recruiting successful . . . an armed force of one regiment or more is necessary. . . . Wherever
we have been able to send a force of 80 or 100 men for a few days into the country, we have
always got men." *Official Records*, III ser., IV: 770.

[29] The battle of Atlanta had been fought only five days earlier, on July 22; but the Confederate forces under General J. B. Hood did not completely evacuate the city until September
1. The news of July 27 of the "capture" of Atlanta was, therefore, premature. Randall,
Civil War, 554.

[30] General J. B. McPherson, one of Sherman's ablest commanders, was succeeded, tem-
porarily, by Major General John A. Logan of Illinois. Within a short time, Major General
O. O. Howard became commander of the Army of the Tennessee. *Ibid.*, 553.

North Bank of Tennessee River in Madison Co. Ala, have been here for Some ten days. The 73 Reg. Vol. inft is here or here and at the several Stockades from here down the River to the mouth of Limestone Creek in Limestone Co. I have been to all those stockades. They are well got up, and as A Reg. the 73 is a fine Jentlemanly and brave set of men well worth there Brave oald State [*Iowa*]. And I am proud to say that I feel under many obligations to the officers and men for there kindness and friendship to me whilst Among them and Especially to Co. I of said Reg. This Co. has one of the best of men for Captain, he is A good officer as well as much of A Jentleman, and there are many of this Co. I shall always Remember with feelings such as I have for A brother or even A Son. I first got acquainted with this Co . out At Stockade at Limestone Bridge on Railroad. They ware garding Road thare and when they were ordered here I Came Along to this place. The assistance this Co. has Rendered me in my Recruiting operations has been valuable for which I feel verry grateful, tho I have not been as Successful as I hoped to be. Still the falt was not theres or mine. Had those officers who are opposed to the inlistment of negroes let me A Lone I should of Raised A fine Lot of niggers here. And then Again as tho this was not Bad Luck Enoughf I was taken sick just when my prospects was best and so Could not opperate for A time. I was seized Last Tuesday morning with a severe Chill Lasting some three hours and then A Raging fever afterwards. Surely I had liked to have went to the Boneyard. One more such Chill and I think I would have got of, But I was well attended to by the skill of that splendid Doctor of this Reg, Miers. Surely this Reg is highly favored and blest in the way of A phasisian not only is he A good skilful Doctor but then he is kind and Affectionate, a thing tho it should be, unfortunately is not always found in Doctors. But Doct. Miers is all of the

Jentleman the Doctor and the good Sameritan nurse. God bless Doctor Miers, and then the Chaplin John Frazer tho peculiar and antick in his ways still I Love him and I believe he is well Received by his Reg, seems to be useful Among the Boys. He hands the Boys out there Rations from Gods word with Earnestness and force and they feel it, for his words have an edge to them. He has Just Commenced A protracted Effort which bids fair so far. God bless the Effort, some forty or more have joined the Union Christian League and we have had some Refreshing times. Lord Convert the intire 73rd Ia. Reg and then they will all be happy, this is my prayer. I find myself today fast Recovering tho weak yet. Hope soon to meet with Conveyance to Huntsville and get straitened up once more. I was Arested while here under the Charge of kidnapping niggers[31] and sent under gard to Huntsville by order of Gen. [*Gordon*] Granger but by showing my papers and making my own Statement assisted by A Letter from Col. R.D. Mussey, They Dismisst the case without trial, so I still Remain in the Boddy, God be praised.   J. T. Ayers.

Wednesday afternoon, Septr 7th 64.

Left Trianna this morning and now am here at Limestone Stockade on Rail Road waiting for the Carrs to pass so I may Reach Huntsville. My health is Rapidly improveing. Soon I hope to be Straight once more. Our means of news is cut off now as the track in several places between here and Nashville is tore up by Wheeler Randy Forest and Co.[32] and there

---

[31] Some commanding officers were opposed to enlistments in the Army by Negroes who were civilian employees in the quartermaster or commissary departments. Although General Sherman had rescinded his order of June 3, 1864, to arrest recruiting agents who did so, Ayers may have been arrested under this order. See *Official Records*, III ser., IV: 434, 436, 454.

[32] Ayers' reference is to Major General Joseph Wheeler's Confederate cavalry raid into east and then middle Tennessee against Sherman's railroad connection to the north, the Nashville and Chattanooga Railroad. Wheeler effected some damage, but his own command had been broken up and scattered. The Union commanders were Brigadier General Robert S. Granger and Major General Lovell H. Rousseau. "Randy" may be Brigadier General Philip D. Roddey who joined with Wheeler in a raid at dawn on Sept. 7. Forest, of course, is Nathan Bedford Forrest.

graceless gang, but I am toald Reausaue and Granger have thrashed them soundly in two battles and Rusau is now in there front and Granger in there Rear and they, the Rebs, are Running and trying to get away. In A day or two the Road will be mended and Trains Running as usual. So All write yet. Shearman I am told has taken Atlanta and with it twelve or fifteen thousand prissoners, hope that may be so. Had no late news from Grant. The wether for sometime past has been Extremely warm here and there has been quiet A number of the Boys down with Chill and fever and Ague and so on, but I hope the worst is over for this year. I feel now much inclined to go to Nashville and throw up my papers and Resign, as I am hartily sick of Coaxing niggers to be Soaldiers Any more. They are so trifleing and mean the dont Deserve to be free. I have often been toald by them when trying to Coax them to inlist, "why" say they "I dont want to be a soaldier."

"Well," say I "you will be made free men Just as soon as you inlist."

"Oh sir," say some "I would rather be A slave all my days than go to war. I cant shoot nor I dont want to shoot Any Boddy. I cant fight."

"Well," say I "we can soon Learn you."

"Yes massa but I have A wife."

"So have we" say I, "and dont you think our wives are as Dear to us as yours are to you?"

"Well, Master, I aint fit for soaldier Any how."

"Well whats the matter?"

"Oh Sir ise Corrupted," meaning Ruptured or "got Rumities or pane in Back or Pneumonia or Arm bent or tooth ache or pain in Ear" or Some Excuse, till I am Hartily sick of hearing them any more and hope to get Dismissed from this Recruiting business. I never have made half Enoughf at it to Pay me for my trouble but still midst all my troubles I must say I have had some Agreeable pleasant seasons, and taking all things as they are I am well Satisfyed. Perhaps I have in this way been of more service to my Country than in Any other way I could have been imployed, so all write.   Jas. T. Ayers.

James T. Ayers, Septr. 9th 64, still at Limestone Bridge.

On the new[s] once more—

Saturday Morning, Septr. 10th 1864

Well I am still here at Limestone Stockade. No trains have passt yet since the Raid. We looked yesterday for A train. Perhaps thare will be one by today. Hope so at least, as I am Anxious to get up to Huntsville and get the news once more. There is now A goodeal of Ague and Chill and fever here Among the Boys. This Limestone Creek is A sickly place tho A Ritch Country of Land. In fact Madison County, Huntsville the County seat and Limestone County, Athens County seat, and Jackson County, Bellfount County seat are all Rich Countyes of Land and the People have here once injoyed great wealth, many of the finest of farms with great nigger quarters Looks Like A little Country vilage forty and fifty buildings Generally in two Rowes with street between of some four or five Rods width with Master's fine big mansion at head of street, About mid way betwean, or Master's great House as the Darkies Call it. This is A fine Cotton Region And fine for Corn, in fact fine for anything but tame grass. It don't do well, to hot and in the Dry hot wether in July and August it Burns out. Blew grass there is none here. This [is] one of the finest places for peaches plums grapes melons and all kinds of fruit. I, the other day, saw several fig trees At Trianna, full of figs. They mostly grow one in A place but occasionally you will see A bunch or Cluster of them togeather. They are About the sise of crabapples and are of A Deep green Coller now. What there coller is when Ripe I can't say. And then the persimmon tree they Abound here and are Loaded this year. They two are About the sise of common Crab Apples and when Ripe are of A Deep brown Purple Coler and are A delishious fruit.   And then here you find the magnolia tree planted here by nature herself as tho oald nature was Determined to Crown with Beauty all its other works in Beauty with this Beautiful tree.   Here she is in all her native glory with her Broad green Leaves her Large big white Roses Look when in full Bloom Like A great white monument handsomely doted with those big green Leaves. Beautiful is the Magnolia tree and those Large fine flowers are of A most Delishious fragrance and Smell.   And here two they Raise the pam Leaf they make hats from.   Indigo Rice sweet potatoes Horses, Cattle, Hogs, Mules, sheep in fact any and Every thing soil Can bring are Raised here.   And here they Raise niggers two by the thousand.   This has been A fine place for Raising woolly heads and seemingly for fear they would not breed fast Enoughf to supply the Demands in there own way the whites, many of them there master at that, have pitched in and help Sambo and Diner Along A little in the Line of Stalk [*stock*] and the Effect is one fourth or say one half of the Darkies ar now a mix⁻ ture of African and white stalk and they have in many instances kept crossing the Blood untill you Could Hardly tell there is Any African there. Some fine Likely Smart women here who are Slaves but thease are mostly owned by Jentlemen for household Servants and wait on Rich oald Betchellors and men tell me they have saw some of those pretty women, slaves I mean, sell at Auction in Huntsville for three thousand.   And in one Case two oald Betchellors were bidding Against Each other for one of those girls to make him a domestick Housekeeper of and She was struck off at 3250 dollars. And Even at that the Auctioneer seemed not Satisfyed, Said he, "Jentlemen its A Shame so fine A looking Girl as this soald for so Small A sum.

She ought to bring five thousand. She is handy Any and every way; washes well A number one seamstress; A good Laundress maker Agreeable and Polite with all, and sound in Lim and Leg. Make A man A snug bedfellow of A coald night. Come up Jentlemen, Examine her, look what fine features, fine Limbs" suiting the Remark with action. "See what A beautiful Leg, did you ever see so fine Smooth A leg hung on a woman," showing her Leg up to her boddy. Just as you or I would A Brute and for the purpose of Exciting the carnal appetite of those Cursed oald Batchellors and get more money Bid. Could Any one Expect anything Else but that God would visit this People for Such sins as thease. Surely God is and will continue to Punish those miserable tirants and Soal killers for there sins. I feel glad in my hart the Cursed thing is winking out and soon the idea of master and slave will be numbered Among the things that was same as oald fashioned witchcraft Among the new Englanders in former day. Lord put the quietus on the Cursed institution and let it go by the Board— I am frequently met in this way, what will become of the niggers if set free they will all Come to want. They wont work without an overseer to drive them. Beside they are so ignorant and stupid they Cant live. They are now better off with there masters than if set free. And you will find it so say the master, and Even others say so. Well my observations this year has Led me fully to the Conclusion that give the nigger his Liberty and A chance in the main they will do well allmost in Every Case. This season in my travels Round Among them to get Soaldiers and being thus imployed I have perhaps more than most of men had an opertunity to see. Those that have got out from under master are, According to there Chance, making good crops of Corn and Cotton and seem to be striving to do as best they can. And my convictions are this that the Slave will Do better without the master than the Master will without the Slave, if there is danger of Starvation in the Premises the Master is the man in danger. This I verily believe true. They are an ignorant people and how Could they be otherwise. We should perhaps be but Little better if Plaiced in there Position. Educate them, set good Examples before them. Let them know they are men and women and are A part and parcel of Gods Creation and I feel Sambo will do tolerably well. Well But if they are set free they will Push into the Northern States and soon they will be in every whole and Corner, and the Bucks will be wanting to galant our Daughters Round. Dam the niggers I would Rather Blow there Brains out than they should do this and so would I. No man would abhor the sight of A big buck nigger leading my daughter or Any white mans Daughter Round than I and yet I think we have ungrounded fears. The niggers place is the South, so gave to him by the All Mighty he is so Constitutionally made, he glorys in the south and Dreads the Coald north, so much so is this the fact that far in the South if you Describe the Place of torment after death as being hot it has no effect to scare those Black skins. But tell them Hell is A place where men freese to death. "Ah, Mister, me nebber wants to go dare." So when this southern Clime is made free these Blacks will never dream of Comeing into our Coald northern Region, no never, not they, but instead there are many now in the North will Come South and I shall find myself grossly Disappointed if in fifty years from this time there was not numbers less of the woolleys in the North than now. Lets try it, we Cant worse ourselves anyhow sure, and so we have nothing to fear and all things to hope for. Much of our Present Difficultyes is to be Attributed to the ministry of the South. "Why, good gracious Mr. Ayers you surely dont mean to say Preachers has had anything to do in bringing those troubles do you? I thought Preachers were to preach the word and warn the People of Danger." "Well I thought so two, in this we Just Agre." "Well tell me what have our Preachers done thats wrong?" "Well, I'll tell you. They have got up into Gods sanctuary on the Sabbath day in the week day, in the day time and at night, and as tho this was not Still Enoughf have mounted the stump and with tears in there eyes toald the People Slaverry was Devine. The[y] have been tryin for A long time to cram Devinity down the throat of slaverry until the People were made to believe A ly through there Lyes and they have hastened the people of the south into madness. Say those Rabbies, "Slaverry always Existed and always will. God sanctioned it, the Saviour Recognized it and so it is Devine," and thus have thease unholy men branded Jehovah with being Partial and unequal in his ways until God has and will wipe them from his foot stool. Look at there churches. Where is the pastor? Look at there flocks, Where are they? Alass all gon Astray. Oh but that this People had know the way and having know, had walked therein, then as A nation our Pace had been as A River and our Righteousness as the waves of the se. Then this most unholy Rebellion would not have taken place. Pastors of the South, I charge you with the inocent blood of many thousands of your brethren that have fallen in Battle. A Rise, shake yourselves, Clear your skirts and warn the People of there danger and of there and your awful sin in Charging God with folly in making Slaverry Devine. You may make slaverry that mans Devises but Dont charge God with making it Devine. Just look at your Churches your farms your flocks all all Deserted and desolate and said the Saviour, "Oh that ye had known this thy day of visitation but now your Houses are left unto your Desolate" etc

When we Remember that this war is for the Petpetuation of Slaverry and its universal Spread all over this fair Land of ours and that the ishue is Slaverry or freedom who for one

moment can Doubt it ishue. It may Last yet for some years.
But I hope not, yey I think not. But still it may Last yet for
some time. God has A great Controversy with this People.
We have all sined before God. God have mercy on us and
save a Remnant of thy People and with them Save this blessed
oald Goverment of our and thease oald Stars and Stripes.
God help them wave from sea to sea, from the Pacific to the
Atlantic, from the Arctic to the Southern Ocean. May the
Stars and Stripes be Reared up and triumphantly wave over
Every Town, Citty and Hamlet in our Land and at mast Head
of Every vesel and on Every fort and in Every Harbour of
North America. So mote it be.   Jas. T. Ayers.

Huntsville Ala, Septr 13th 1864.
    This morning finds me here at this place. There is Con-
siderable of Stir Among the troops here. They are mostly
going East now. A few days since between five and ten thousand troops went west to head or help to head Wheeler And
Co. Who was making A Raid on our Rail Road Leading from
Decature to Nashville and they played Smash with the Road
in several places.[33] So we have had no trains in from North
since and Consequently have had now Reliable news, but I
learn the Road is now Ready for trains once more and there
will be a train in from Nashville this Evening. Wont there be
A big Rush for Papers! I hope to get some letters then. Have
had none for A long time. I am sending now letters as follows by next mail to Smalley, Fulwiler, Walton, Susan Ayers,
Permelia S. Ayers, Miss Martha Davis. Have lately sent Joseph
Ayers, Henry Ayers, Robert M. Vance, John Warick, Squire
Beach, and John Casady letters and had as yet no Answers. I
am getting Prety stout once more. This is Lovely fine wether
here now. We have good news from Shearman, he has At-

[33] See note 32, page 45, for Wheeler's raid into middle Tennessee.

lanta. We have no news yet from General Grant. Hope to get word from him when trains Arive from Nashville. My Private opinion is that this cursed Rebellion is mostly played out Especially if our fall Election goes off write. If we Elect Father Abraham and Johnson it will settle the question. The South will See no more hopes of making Capital in the North, and I think they will begin to Look things squarely in the face which I am satisfyed they would have done Long since had they not been promised help from the North by such men as Velandingham, Long, Voheese, Buel and others Like them selves.[34] But if those Peace Candidates are Defeated this fall the thing will be settled in my opinion for surely they the south know well as we and even better that they cant hoald out four years more. They are prety well whittled up now. Lets Look at them for A moment. How does matters Stand now to what they did in the beginning of Rebellion. They Had the navy the money the arms all in there hands. They had Virginia, Meriland, Tennessee, Missouri, and we might say Kentucky also, for all the benefits she has been to us and how is it now in those four years. We started At the Ohio River a[t] Louisville, Cincinnati, Pittsburg. This was our Base, then How now we are all over Alabam, Georgia, Missippi, Louisanna, Arkansas, Texas, and have taken Kentucky, Missouri, Tennessee, Meriland, and part of Virginia, and our Base now far Down in Georgia and while they have got there Last man in the field to as best they Could hoald us at bay this summer and fall till after Elections hoping for A devishion in the North.

[34] Clement L. Vallandigham, of Ohio, regarded as the leader of the "Copperheads" of the Northwest, had been instrumental in forcing into the Democratic platform of 1864 a resolution declaring the war a failure and demanding an immediate cessation of hostilities.

Alexander Long, congressional representative from Ohio, had demanded disunion and peace.

Daniel Voorhies ("The Tall Sycamore of the Wabash") was a Democratic Congressman from Indiana during the war, and one of the foremost critics of the Lincoln administration.

General Don Carlos Buell ranked in the minds of many Northerners with George B. McClellan as a man of no action.

We are Just now getting A good Ready and the Next four years we shall be in better trim for fighting   have more men in the field than ever before.   In fact the true Strength of the government is only Just beginning to show itself.   The South see all this well as we.   They aint A sleep.   All in the world that has made this war Linger thus far has been this Howl in the North by this Peace Party.   If they are handsomely beaten this fall A settlement will be made.   I feel sure of this.   Then Give us Father Abraham and Andy and all will be write but if this Peace party does prevail we are all gon to the Devil head long sure and certain in my mind.   God forbid they should prevail. Well I am so tired of nigger Recruiting I am going as soon as A train goes through to Nashville to Resign and Go back to my Reg. or try.   Jas. T. Ayers.

Sunday Morning October 9th 1864
    Well here am I at Chatanooga.   It was Coald as Greenland Last night, ground frose and ice plenty.   Stayed at soaldiers Home.   Came here last Evening on train from Nashville and am on my way to my Regiment, but cant proceed any farther for the present as the Road Leading from here to Atlanta is for some distance tore up by the Rebs.   I may have to stay here for A week or more, but what of that.   I am living well here.   Get A Rasher of Raw fat sowbelly, A slice of soft Bread and A tinfull of Coffee at A meal and Am getting fat on it. Oh it is glorious for A Soaldier.   Chatanooga is not so large A place as I Expected to see, Rather unsightly at that.   It is on the south Bank of the Tennessee River and in the Edge of the State of Tens.   I left Huntsville last Wednesday at 2 O'cl p.m. Oct 5th by way of Stevenson for Nashville and Oh But I had A Sweet time. I had to go on frait train Loaded with Indianna soaldiers going home to vote at State Election and our carrs ware oald Leaky Ricketty Cattle carrs nee deep or Less in Cow

dung and it having rained day and night for sometime Previous and Still Raining it had this manure in fine trim, just mellow Enoughf to be spungy. We got an oald nigger to scrape some of the top off and this Raised the smell to About forty five or fifty Blood heat, no seats no dodging no let up and here we went. Got to Stevenson at ½ past 8 p. m. and then was toald that the same train would Start at 10 P. M. for Nashville and so we staid A Board. Here we got Some billets of wood and threw in to sit on and at one o'clock A.M. Away we went. Sure enoughf out we goes Like A scird dog for six mortal miles and switched off and lay here till sunrise. Then off again   switching off at nearly every Station on the way for down trains to pass us and so Arive safe and sound in Nashville next morning At one o'clock A.M. being two nights and one and half days in said trip, setting & Standing as the Dutchmans blue hen did. Well that passt of and all over. Had a good time Comeing from Nashville here. Rode in A private carr and faired Like an oald coon. This is A beautiful morning now, Clear and warming up A little. My health I find is Rapidly on the improve. Hope I shall soon be all write once more. While at Nashville I saw Mr. Wheeler[35] and got 150 dollars out of him, had got 65 before so as the oald saying is A half Loaf is better than no Bread, but White is gon so I loose all that. On the 7th inst I Expresst Joe from Nashville $200.00 in care of Grid and sent Joe A letter telling him of it. Shall send Henry a letter today.   J. T. Ayers.

Still At Chatanooga Oct. 12th 64.
    Nothing of great interest to Record now. Wether fine Everything Livly Round here. This is A Novel Place. Setting in the window as I am up Stairs at soaldiers Home I look out North East from here say half mile thare is a great big fort

---

[35] This Mr. Wheeler is probably the same one referred to by Ayers on p. 1.

and directly East near same distance is an other fort and then
North is another or Rather three of them all large forts.   In
fact this is A citty of Forts surrounded in all Directions only
West and there is two prety fair forts here and then Close by
on my west here I see the East end of Lookout Mountain pok-
ing her Great high head Above the Clouds nearly into the
Citty as much as to say, "I am oalder and biger than you are,
Mr. Citty."   And so she is and I tell you she Carrys A high
head and Looks like A great Monster as she is.   Chatanooga
is not verry slightly it being two much scattered Round and
two irregular tho I see some fine buildings here, but ware it
not for the mountains and peaks here which are all Round in
full Sight thare would be nothing verry inviting here to draw
the attention of the visitor.   There is A considerable Amount
of soaldierry here in those forts and Spread Round.   I am not
Posted to know how many there is, quiet a number of officers
and soaldiers here waiting with as much patience as is posable
to get front and join there Regiments but we must wait yet for
a while as the Rebs have tore up the Road from here front in
several places and so destroyed the Road that carts cant get to
Atlanta.   Yet we all hope thad in a day of two we may get
through.   Well since I Came here we have had several Evening meetings which seemed to be quiet interesting and if the
wether still Should be favourable I feel some good will Result
from those meetings.   We hoald them out doores and if it
should Rain and get muddy we shall have to Close.   We have
those meetings Every night and will have one to night if all is
favourable but it now Looks as tho we shall have A Rainey
night.   I came here saturday afternoon Last.   Am still slowly
on the improve tho am much troubled with my Urine, having
to wait on it About once an hour day and night so it Disturbs
me in my Rest.   Perhaps if it Rains and stops our meeting I
may get better as I presume my Exertions at said meetings

fatigue greatly as I am weak yet. There was A case of small pox broke out in our Room today and Caused some Excitement for A while but the sufferer is Removed and all wags on once more. More Anon. Jas. T. Ayers.

Once more And Still At Chatanooga.
Sunday morning Oct. 16th A.D. 1864.

We are having some verry stiring times All Round here. The whole Rebel Army is making in this way and we looked [for]them here. General Stanley[36]Received orders to Rally arm And put Every man here. Convalessence and all, all such as Could walk A mile, into Ranks and station at and Round Forts, Rifle pits and trenches so as to be Ready at A minutes warning in Case of an Attact. I tell you this caught up hundreds that was here playing off to keep from front. Beside there was A Large Crowd here Like myself but cut off so we could not get to our Reg, so we have had A Big time sure as Life. Those who had no Arms all drew arms and such as had no tents Drew those Little Pup or Dog tents as the Boys call them. I drew A gun catridge Box Belt and trimmings and me and A Mr. Bradt of Wisconsin Drew one of those little fellers of the Pup Stalk [stock] in cahoot And have just got it up and I am sitting in it now writing all the scattered fragments of the several Regiments Composing or that belonged to the 20eth Army Corpse ware threw into A company numbering some forty odd and we are Co. B and so all the Different Corpses was organized similar and Lettered and here we are Chuerned all up Like Aunt Sallys Buttermilk and how Long we may have to stay is hard to tell, tho I think But for A few days. It is said

---

[36] The account of these events is given by Major General D. S. Stanley in his report to the Chief of Staff, Brigadier General W. D. Whipple, February 25, 1865. *Official Records*, I ser., XXXIX, pt. 1: 907-08. The Confederate forces in northern Georgia and Alabama under Hood, after the loss of Atlanta, attempted to break Sherman's communication lines to Chattanooga and Nashville. Eventually Hood moved his forces westward and embarked upon his disastrous campaign which ended with his defeat by Thomas at Nashville, December 15, 1864.

this morning that the Rebs are turning now towards Knoxville. They came within Some 20 miles of here and have taken several Considerable places on Rout from here to Atlanta, Dalton for inst and so on which made it Prety Exciting here. Our officers and Attachees ware all flying Round day and night, men in all Directions on the march to there several Posts, some with guns some with Spades some with picks and those who had no Arms ware organised marched off in squads by officers to Arsenal to Draw Arms.   Men Ariving from Trains Every hour or two taking all in all things looked Prety Lively for three days, but are Rather quieting down A little now and Large train Loads are yesterday afternoon throug the night and this forenoon moveing front Again to Look for Burygard [*Beauregard*] and Co. Shearman we understand is Close in his Rear. We shall have A big fight somewhere near here soon, no mistake of that. Boath Armys are trying to get an Advantage in Some way and must Soon Come togeather and then Blood must Run Freely. We are in the front, Rear and on Either side of them in heavy force, and while they have and will still do us much Injury Still I think there fate is sealed. Not one half of them will never make there Escape if Any does. I find my self still weak tho some on the gain. We are having fine wether here now which is Luck for us if it was A rainey time with those Little tents we would suffer. Well I'll close this Epistle now and tell the balance next time.

Oct. 16th 64   Jas. T. Ayers.

Friday afternoon, Oct. 21st 1864

We are Still here in Camp Close by East end of Lookout Mountain. We are on [*the*] big Mountain Close by side of A fort to support it.   In the Bottom Below us and near the River is four or five Regiments in Camp or tent as we are. Just Acrost the River in A Large field is A Large Drove of beef cattle. Thare was A gun Boat Came puf pufing up the River Last Evening and Laid here Close by us Last night and this morning on She went plowing her way up Amidst the Strong Current here. The River has A verry Strong Current here in those mountains. We are having fine wether here now, tho some cool at night, and we have had A hard time so far for wood, Sciercely being Able to pick up A sufficiency to Cook our Little meals. But the worst is over I hope in this way as we got Some 12 or more Loads good wood hawled to us this morning. We Seem to have Rather A fair set of officers and all seems to wag on Prety fair. We have good news from Sheridan this morning. He has Licked Longstreet,[37] taken many prisoners Burnt and Captured A large portion of his train and Captured 43 of his Cannon. Hurrah for Sheridan. I have had several meetings here in Battalion. Will have one tonight if nothing Special to hinder. I feel I shall be useful here. God help, and bless the Efforts. Bless thy Cause, bless our Union and help Drive out Rebellion. Jas. T. Ayers.

Chatanooga, October 25th 64.

This is A beautiful pleasant morning. Nature seems in her best mood and we feel to Rejoice at the Rumer this morning Afloat that Shearman met Hood And Co. yesterday And whiped him soundly Scattering the whole Army in all Directions, Completely Demoralised, we hope it may be so. I have been Greatly under par for several weeks. The Effects of Chill and fever I caught up in Alabama swamps, but I feel so much better this morning I fear I am not as thankful as I should be to my heavenly father. I think now in A few days I'll get off for My Reg. at Atlanta. There are five of us here Detailed and Left here to gard the Bagage of Headquarters as the Bat-

---

[37] General Phil Sheridan, on October 19, made his famous ride from Winchester, rallied his Army of the Shenandoah at Cedar Creek, Va., and snatched victory from defeat. Jubal A. Early, not James Longstreet, had been the Confederate commander.

tallion has moved front so we Stay and go by Rail when it is Repaired. Boys are shaving this morning and all gay and Gleeful.   Jas. T. Ayers.

Oct. 28th 64,[38] And still another Letter on the N[ews]

I left Chatanooga friday at 2 O'clock p.m. for Nashville. There was say three or three hundred and fifty of us Convalescents and we was promised Hospital Carrs but when we Came to Depoe we found A train in Readiness for us made up of oald Ricketty Stalk cars tore full of holes and with all quiet Stinking at that and A few oald plank benches in them for seats and not half Enoughf of them for sit on. So many had to sit on the flore or Stand as best they could and we traveled all night Reaching Nashville next morning Oct. 29th at 6 A. M. The night was coald and carrs so open and all of us in pore health we suffered with coald. We was met at Nashville by some men who was ordered to see us and marched off to several Different Hospitals in Different squads, me and my squad going to No. 8 near Post office and ajoining Zolacoffer House. Here we was taken up in the 5th Story and stayed untill Monday Morning Oct. 31st. Then some thousand of [or] fifteen hundred marched down to Louisville Depoe and Cared up by the Doctors for this place. We had a good time Comeing from Nashville here Ariving here at 6 P. m. Last Evening and found in waiting Ambulance Drivers and men waiting to take us all to places prepared for our Accommodations. So Away we went, found kind friends good suppers, good Bunks, good Breakfast and are now only waiting our Transportation Papers which will soon be Ready and then Away we'll all go for our several homes Joyous at the Idea of once more getting permitted to imbrace our friends and see oald America having been so long down

---

[38] This entry must have been written a day or two later.

Amidst those sour faced shea and hea Devils in Shape of Human form one gets tired. Well tho I have quiet A Severe Disinterry still I feel tolerably well. This morning it is Cloudy and quiet coald here for the season. I hope we shall Leave here at 2 O'clock p.m. and then For voting. Well my vote will be cast if I live for Father Abraham For President and Andy for vice President and Oglesby[39] for Govenor and in short my vote will be Union all through sure as life.   Jas. T. Ayers.

I want to say that I have say fifty dollars worth of Books at Mrs. Gennings in Nashville on Currey Street near fire Engine No. five and Hospital No. one in South part of Citty and A gun and all the Equipments for it at Hospital No. 8 at Nashville Just west of Zolacoffer House and near Post office, also close the St. Cloud Hotell up in fifth story of said building.
                                        J. T. A.

And Mr. White Agrees to Collect for Me 128 dollars for my Recruiting 64 negroes and Deposit in Nashville Bank for me to my order.   J.T.A.

[*Ayers' next entry is obviously written at his son-in-law's house in Fairbury, Illinois.*]

Nov. 10th A.D. 1864—John Waricks[40] House.

I came here Last friday Evening in Rout and on 20 days furlow from Chatanooga which place I left on Last friday week. I landed in Fairbury Thursday evening Nov. 3rd at 5 o'clock p.m. and we had a fine snow that night covering the ground some five inches Deep, but it has all Disappeared and we have had quiet A Rainey time since up till yestarday afternoon. It turned coald and wind blew A perfect gale all night,

---

[39] Major General Richard J. Oglesby, of Decatur, Illinois, had distinguished himself as a military leader in the early days of the war. As chairman of the state Senate committee to reorganize the militia in 1861 he predicted that "the whole country . . . would rise *en masse*, and . . . volunteer their services . . . speedily and without delay." A. C. Cole, *The Era of the Civil War* (Springfield, 1919), 273, 328.

[40] John Warick lived in Fairbury, Illinois, where Ayers owned property.

But has Layed Down now and to night is fine, moon shines and has some the appearance of being fine weather now. Hope it may as the farmers are only Just Commenced there Corn geathering here. On Sundy Morning Nov. 6th my suninlaw and Daughter presented me with A little stranger in the shape of A grand Daughter. All partyes so far seem to be getting A long finely. The little stranger once and A while joging our memory she is here by her Little inocent Cryes which is Common in all such cases. I this day have soald My oald Homestead place to Sam A. Vance for fifteen hundred dollars, five down five hundred Septr next five hundred Septr Come year with six per cent interest from date. I still find my health quiet pore, hope I shall soon be better. Balance next time.

Jas. T. Ayers.

At John Warick's Sunday Morning Nov. 13th 64.

I am Still here at my Soninlaws. This is A beautiful morning after Such A big Storm. All nature seems to be Smiling and Joyous. The Earth is crowned with Hoary frost this morning. On Last thursday night we had quiet A snow Storm but it soon disappeared. Verry little done yet in the way of Corn geathering in these parts. Health here Generally good. Country all in A flourishing State, Money plenty, Stalk [stock] high, Land on the Rise Rapidly. All out on the track for money making but amidst all this what creatures of sorrow and affliction we are. I had but Just got Home Amidst my friends and children when my Daughter was confined and Has A Little Daughter born Nov. 6th Since that time She my Daugter has been in A critical State of health, part of her time intirely Devoid of her Reason and Still Remains So yet, tho I feel some hope she is some better. We had A Doctor here with her Last night. I did intend Starting yesterday for Josephs[41] but postponed going in Consequence of the above

---

[41] Joseph was Ayers' son. He then lived in the western part of McLean County, Illinois.

sickness. Hope I may get off tomorrow. I have imployed Doctor Fulton to Extend My furlow for thirty days Longer which will Run untill 20eth December. I trust I shall be well by that time. We have Just got the Glorious news that Lincoln is Elected President By an overwhelming Majority, Leaving Pore Little Mack[42] far in the Rear and as harmless to us now as he was to the Rebs when he was so snugly stowed away on the Gunboat. Pore little feller, we'll ask him in when we want him. I have Just soald my oald Home Stead for $1,500 dollars, put my five Lots in Fairbury in Judge Mcdowells hands for sale at 60 dollars per Lot making $300 dollars more. Shall have five hundred dollars worth Rent Corn. Joseph has three hundred and sixty dollars Cash of mine. White owes me $128[43] dollars, the Goverment Does and will owe me first Septr next $75 dol. Bounty Warant for 160 Acres Land and two hundred and thirty eight dollars for my pay at $16 per month, all puted up as now out standing is as follows to Wit: Look above on other Page.

$3101.00) beside I hoald Downings notes for $75.00 note or Rather Account now was A note but Henry Lost said note on Barnam of Chetworth[44] Livingston Co. for $15 dollars and Wesley Huston owes me ten dollars cash borrowed money making $100 more Aded is Thus $3201.00. Well here I'll close. Jas. T. Ayers.

I owe Wm. Cowan	$60.00
Hen McKey	10.00
A man at Chenoah	22.00
McCurday	

---

[42] General George B. McClellan, the Democratic candidate for President.

[43] Ayers' compensation as a recruiting agent is here partly indicated. He had been designated a recruiting agent, and here admits that his pay was the $16 per month of a private soldier. The $128 he claimed for recruiting 64 Negroes (see p. 61), but from what funds it was to be paid is not made clear, nor why he was claiming the $75 bounty warrant.

[44] Chatsworth, Ill.

And Straight at Fair-   15.00
                bury

———————

$107.00

This is all I owe in this world. This is A faithful schedule of my Effects and my indebtedness. Besides I have at the Citty of Nashville fifty or sixty dollars worth Books Left at Mrs. Gennings in South part of Citty on Cherry Street Near Engine No. 5 and Hospital No. one. There is also A Saloon and news Depot near her Residence. Her Residence is on write side of Street as you goe South. I feel this morning some on the improve thank God.   Jas. T. Ayers.

Wednesday Morning, Nov. 23rd 64.

Well I have been down to My sons in West part of Mclean Co. Found him and his family in Reasonable health and in fine Spirits. Joseph is making money fast, has A fine Crop this year and A nice Lot of Cattle and Hogs on hand feeding and has A good Lot of Horses. Prety well over with his Corn geathering for this fall. I left there on Last friday Nov 18th and Arived at Waricks on Saturday forenoon. Found Mrs. Warick Dangerously Sick and Deprived of her Reason. We have had Doctors Watters Hulsey and Fulton in attendance and have made all Exertions posable for her Re-coverry but all seemingly so far to little Purpose. The Case Still seems Doubtful and I have but Little Hope of her Re-coverry. We have been having some Coald Chilly wether for the Last few days past but is this morning more pleasant. I find that not withstanding I have much fatigue and Loss of sleep with my watching with Mrs. Warick Still my health is on the improve thank God and I Earnestly Hope that in A few days Sarah may be better so I may Leave Again for the Army as I shall go so soon as I can Leave. I have seen Henry and he was well and now is in Chicago Ills Attending the medical Lectures thare. God bless our Nation our Armies the President the Generals and all our Union officers and Soaldiers and save our oald Goverment is my prayer. J.T.A.

WHERE IS GOD IDE LIKE TO KNO

(Where is God Ide like to kno)
1 If he's here in this world of wo
  If Earth Contains Gods presence why
  Do men shed each others Blood and Dy

2 Surely Gods presence is everwhare
  His works and wisdom this declare
  Mans the monster, not God
  Our hands are swift to shed mans blood

3 Gods will to men is Joy and Peace
  Its Gods Good pleasure Strife Should cease
  And when we fall at Jesus feet
  War will end and Peace be Sweet.

4th Lord send the welcome tidings down
  Dispatch A herald newly Crownd
  To Sound the news from shore to Shore
  That war has ceased to Rise no more.

5th My Prayer Oh Lord my God Shall be
  That all mankind may be set free
  Set free from Tyrannyes Rod
  Made free in Christ to Live with God.

Written and Composed by J. T. A. for Miss Theressa Hamilton by her Request to place in her Album.

Nov. 26th A. D. 1864 while at my Daughters who is lying at the Point of Death. God be merciful to us spare her Life if it is thy will, But if she must Dy Lord Save her in thy Kingdom.

The answer to the above Lines will be found on other side of Page.   Jas. T. Ayers.

God is here and Every whare
His sacred word does this Declare
His Kingdoms vast and has no bound
Angelic Hosts do him Surround

2nd The Sun and Moon and Stares in fine
Proclaim Gods work to be Divine
Heaven and Earth and Man declare
Gods presence is Every whare.

3rd The Different Seasons of the year
The wisdom of there God Declare
Wisely has God made Spring and fall
To bless the Nations great and Small.

4th Summer and winter two we see
Are here Arrangeed as they Should be
The Summers warm which yields the fruit
So needed for Boath Man and Brute.

5 Every thing seems to off had Design
There Maker Surely was Divine
Divine and Skilful two was he
To make those beauties here we see.

6th How thankful then ought we to be
And praise this Heavenly Deity
Who to us has been so good
As to save our Soals in Christ our Lord.
                                    Jas. T. Ayers.

Tuesday Nov. 29th 64.

I find Mrs. Waric Some better to day tho Still partially in A State of Mental Derangement. The Doctor has been here today and Seems now to have Some hope. The wether is warm now and verry pleasant. Everyboddy Busily Corn geathering, women and all. Corn A little down Just now, only sixty cents in market, was Last week 85 cents. Horses Hogs Cattle and Merchandise all up verry high. Land has Ris also Double to what it was four years since. If I live and no Accident I shall Start front on thursday Dec. 15th which is day after tomorrow two weeks.   Jas. T. Ayers   at Waricks.

Dec. 7th A.D. 1864

Well it Snowed night before last so as to Cover the ground and was Rather Coald yestarday. Last night snowed again, so we have this morning A prety fair sledding snow. Wind blows to day and Snow Drifts and flyes finely. I have now been over four weeks housed up at Waricks nursing my Daughter and find her now but little better, still in A State of Derangement. My own health is now good, nothing new on hand, so I close.   J. T. Ayers.

[*The next entries were written after Ayers had left Illinois to join his company in Savannah, Georgia.*]

Dec. 31st 1864, Near Harisburg, Pa.

Well I'll commence my Epistle. I left Fairbury on thursday Dec. 16th and on Sunday morning at 7 O'clock Landed at Nashville Tenn. We had some delay on Rout on the account of A train Running off Just Ahead of us Saturday Evening six miles North of Nashville and we had to Lay by all night on Train so Reached Nashville as stated. I Reported to Hospital as ordered and Stayed thare untill Tuesday. On tuesday Morning when the Doctor Came Round to Examine us all I reported myself Able for light Duty and in Afternoon was notifyed to Report at Baracks, No. one, which is the Big Zolacoffer House and when I got there I found six or seven thousand soaldiers stored Away in the various Rooms of this building Like so many porkers. Here we got two meals per day and only About half Enoughf At that and Gards plaiced over us so no one Could get out of this place of torment. If Hell is Any worse than this place God have mercy on us pore creatures and save us from going thare. And in the midst of all our troubles as tho being garded Like A set [of] fellons by the meanest pack God ever made here we found the graybacks thick as hale and big Enoughf to plow with had they been Harnessed up. Taking all in all I hope in God never to see Zoli-coffer Again. Well we Recvd orders from Sherman to Hasten to his Command[45] and on Saturday morning Dec 24th we bid Adieu to this Cursed place, 200 of us and carred up for Louisville and Away we go glad that We had made our Escape from those infernal Regions of woe and miserry, but Little thinking we ware still doomed to Disappointment for we was thinking and talking merily of our big Christmas Dinner in Louisville, but when we Reached Mumfordsville we ware toald that General Lyons[46] with his Rebel gang had Burned A Large bridge Captured A train in Advance of us and 200 or more of our soaldiers. So we halld up and Stayed here until Monday taking our Christmas on hard tack and sow belly. After diner Monday we set out once more and soon came to the scene of Destruction—Bridges Burned down Carrs all burned and standing on track River up high and we was put to our trumps to Cross. But necessity is always the mother of invention so we invented A way of crossing and got over by felling trees Each way and then piling rails on top and thus made a kind of Bridge And footed it for About one mile and found A train waiting for us. So all Abord Again for Louisville and Landed thare that night And Marched to Baracks No. one or Exchange Baracks. Here we stayed untill the next evening and then Crosst over into America or Jeffersonville Indianna. Here we soon got on train and Away for Indianapolis, Landing thare at three o'clock next morning Dec. 28th. Stayed here untill 6 O'clock A.M. 29th and then cared up for Cresline by way of Bellfountain Ariving at Cresline at some ten o'clock at night. Here we Laid in the Cares we Came in untill morning Dec 30eth, then the iron horse Cam prancing and snorting up to our Carrs and hitched two and Away we go Again. I for-

---

[45] General Sherman had captured Savannah and established his headquarters there, December 22, 1864. His Army had "marched to the sea" from Atlanta since November 10.
[46] Brigadier General Hylan B. Lyon.

got to tell you it Turned Coald on our way from Jeffersonville to Indianapolis and A small Sprinkle of snow fell and has been Coald Ever since. And as we advanced the Debth of the snow increased and as the snow increased the Coald increased in proportion. Well I said we Left Cresline for Pittsburg, Pa. Reaching thare after night A little and here we was met and Conducted to soaldiers Home and had A sumptuous supper Provided for us and being Hungary we surely acted our part and went in with A will. I most assuredly would do Pittsburg injustice ware I to omit saying that we were better treated and met A kinder Reception than at Any other Place on whole Rout. Well we Left Pittsburg for Harisburg the Capital of Penn and then from thare to Philadelphia. Here we got some Refreshments tho Rather Pore and from here we took train sixty miles Through Jersey and then unshiped and took A steamer and on Last Evening Jan 1st we Landed here at New York. We made our way to baracks and here we are Doing prety well this Jan 2nd 65. Taking all things as they are we have great Reason to be thankful to our Heavenly Father for his kindness to us. We had no Accident on the way tho we suffered from Coald and some for Rest and so on and many of us have Caught bad Coalds. Still no one has gave out None Cripled and all seem Cherful and gay. God bless the soaldier. I'll write the balance when we Land at Savanna as we will Start in A day or two. Jan 2nd A.D. 1865.   Jas. T. Ayers.

Jan. 12th 1865
    On the New[s] at Savanna Georgia.
    Well we Stayed at those Barack untill Jan 3rd. In the Evening we was ordered into Rank and Oh but it was snowing and blowing At A merry Rate. Well we marched to the Ship Landing and was Shiped for Governors Island Just over yonder and Away we went and when Landed, was Again marched

to Casle Williams, A place I never want to see Again while I Remain in the flesh. Here we was forced in for we had to force nature to get in in the first place and then force nature to indure it in the next place needeep or Less in Dirt and filth and Stunk worse than A desent hog pen, beside Graybacks thick as hale and Large Enoughf for oxen had they of been yoked up, that is the masterly ones. The General herd was Rather small and Lean, being so numerous I suppose was the Cause. Well here we crowded in, Coald night no fire no supper no No Breakfast. In fact, In my former, I said if Hell was Any worse than the Zollacoffer in Nashville God pitty us and Save us from Going thare, but Casle William is Still Several Degrees worse and to still add to our pain, of all Gods Creation Surely those that manage this infernal whole are the meanest. I suppose tho that they they have been so Annoyed with those bounty Jumpers and Conscripts, and Rakings of all Gods Creation and then there Stomachs have Lately been so cloged with the numerous herd of Copperheads that so numerously infest this Copperhead Citty. No wonder they they treated us as they did. They have so Long associated with Demons and snaks they have lost all feelings of men and seem to possess the feelings of Brutes. Well long have I herd of the great Citty of New York but if what I saw and indured thare is Anything of A fair Specimen of her Common Hospitality and Refinement I hope to be Excused. One would Suppose that so great a Citty as this would and Could have fed Housed and taken better Care of A Small handful of war worn veteran western Soaldiers, but Alass for her She is so full of Poision, Like Snakes in Dogdays, she seems to have Lost all feelings of Decency and Common Humanity, and her Snakeship only thinks of Bountys, Bounty Jumping McClelling Copperheadism, and Valandigam Thunder Hammer toryism or some kind of Devilism. Well New York Thou great Citty of Harlots tho thou Exalt thyself up to Heaven thou shall be thrust down to Hell. Well on Thursday 2 O'clock P.M. of Jan. 5 we ship Aboard of A Large propeller 500 of us stored Away Close as swine or Sheep on Cares Down in the whole of this vessel and Away we go for Hilton Head and for five Mortal days and nights our Little Giant vessel pufft and Blowed and Sped Away on oald Ocean all seeming to bid fair for our safety only many of the boys was verry sea sick and such ooping and yorking as was on Board I never before had seen as I never before traveled on the mighty Deep. But Amidst all the sea Sickness on Board thank God I Escaped being sick in the Least. Well on Saturday night Jan 7th we ware overtaken by A ferful Storm which made our vessel Real and stagger Like a Drunk Man and Every Joint in her Crack and tremble, and for A while we knew not but that Every moment might be our Last and we all imbrace one Common grave at the Bottom of this the Father of Watters. But thanks be to God for his goodness and watchful care who hoalds the winds in his hand he said, "Peace be Still," and our Little giant Steamer that had so masterly Rode through this Mighty Storm once more moved Smoothly over the serface and on Tuesday 12 we Landed safe at Hilton Head Late in the Evening. Here we unshiped and Reshiped Aboard of two small Steamers as one was not sufficiently Large to Carry us all and passt out into the sea some distance cast anchor and Layed by untill morning. Then Away we go once more passing various Little places we Could see on shore untill we Reached Beaufort.[47] Here we Came two and all the soaldiers of 15th and 17th Army Corpse ware Landed at this place as there corpses were here and the Remainder of us were kept on Board. Here we Lay all night and on next morning Jan. 12th we Rolled out for Thunderboalt,

[47] Hilton Head Island, S. C., is between the mouth of the Savannah River and the entrance to Port Royal Sound. Beaufort, S. C., is above Port Royal on the Beaufort River, which flows into Port Royal Sound.

a fortification on Savannah River five or six miles from the
Citty of Savanna Reaching here Late in the Evening of same
day. Here we Landed and Disembarked. Here it seemed to
me the world was full of Blue coats before behind and all
Round, nothing to be seen only Blue coats waggons and teams
and Cavalry beside two large Steamers Loded with Blue Coats
Bound for Buford and I understand the Largest Portion of
this whole Army is and soon will be on its way thither prepara-
tory to another important move, perhaps on Charleston. Well
we got in Double file and About sundown Rolled out Afoot
Back for Savanna. Reached there in Safety and after some
trouble and delay was conducted to United States Barack
where we stayed untill morning. After we had Eat some Hard
tack and Devoured our Last of sowbely we was put in Rank
and Each man Calld on for his name Reg. Co. and Corpse and
each squad sent Amediately to his Corpse thence to his Division thence his Brigade thence to his Reg. and after Passing
through all those ordeals we Rolled up to Co. E. Mike Morris
and myself having traveled all the Round togeather from
Nashville here. And after passing through so many Adventures and saw so many Novel and Strange sights as we did had
we only of had a Robison Cruso or a Sinbad to pen our Adventures down as they occured with the Exception of the
Great Snake story we far Exceeded them and even with his
Snake in the pile, we nearly match him or them for we saw on
Saturday hundreds of great Sea Horses Rising fare up in sight
in there Sportive play Running after Around and even Passing
us. Thease sea monsters are verry Large and are queer Looking Customers and while they were Sporting and Raring as
they did the Sailors said we would have A storm and So it was.
How those creatures know before of an Approaching Storm is
hard to tell but it seems they do or the saylors Say they always
take those plays Just before A big storm and in this case it so

turned out at Least. Well While on this great Water tossing from side to side, Sea Roaring, winds Howling, wave surging, foam boiling, men heaving and vomiting, Captain giving orders, Sailors flying from post to Post to obey orders I could but think of Moses Account of the mighty flood and Says Moses "the Fountains of the Great Deep were broken up and the windows of Heaven were opened." It seemed to me on this occasion that oald ocean was most as sick as we, trying to Roll inside out and tho it Rained not as in the days of the flood, Still it Rained and surely the winds blew at A Desperate Rate. Well in Gods Great mercy I find myself once more on Tereferma and the nex Ride I take make A Land seafairing trip whare it is easier to Cast anchor Especially whare the mud is prety deep. Well I find 129th[48] incamped on an oald farm Close by an oald family semetry Called the Hardee farm and Hardee semetry. This is A Little Rising from the Common Level of surrounding Country and is beautiful Handsomely sourrounded on all Sides with Large tall Straight pine trees and Live oak Timber. Some of those Live oaks are here in Edge of the incampment and are as green as midsummer. Finally, the senery Round here is beautifully grand even beyond Description. Boys all seem in fine Health and high glee. God be praised. I'll Close this now.

Well here we are at Hardeeville South Carolina, A little vilage some 20 miles North East of Savanna Georgia, Jan. 17th 65.

We Received marching orders yestarday afternoon. We ware Laying at fortress Hardee ten or twelve miles from here between this and Savanna. We was to be packed up and

---

[48] This is the regiment to which Ayers was originally attached when he volunteered in 1862, the 129th Infantry, Illinois Volunteers. Ayers had enlisted when it was organized in August, 1862. He had been assigned to Company E, which was made up of Fairbury men. The regiment had operated first in the west, and then as part of the 20th Corps of Sherman's Army during the campaign for Atlanta and on the march to the sea. It was to continue with Sherman through the Carolinas until the end of hostilities.

Ready for move at ½ past 7 A. M. so when all packed up Boys all Set fire to there Camps and thare was two Large farm buildings within Presincts of incampment of our Brigade They also was fired and the boys had A gay oald time. The sene was beautifully grand to see the burning Camps the burning b u i l d i n g s was to me a grand sight. Well we marched off and took road for Hardeeville and on way thare was several buildings burned or set on fire and Left in flames.—Such is the feelings of the officers and Soaldiers that not many buildings or Stalk [*stock*] or anything we or they the Rebs can use will be left on our Rout.[49] Well when we Came to Hardeeville we Halted and will stay here At least over night and may Stay A day or two here. Thare is quiet A number of frame buildings, some prety good. Well the Brigade was Each Redgiment marched to Different parts of this place and Slung knapsac or unslung and then you had better believe the Boys went in with A will. I never saw the Like before. In Less than half hour all those buildings ware tore down and piled in Rowes Ready to convert into Camps for Each Company. This being done then we Took the S[*h*]ingles and slivered planks and frames made fires and in no time was sipping Away at our Hot Coffee mixing up A little with Hard tack and sowbelly as composed as tho Hardeeville was Still Standing and in her great Glory. I was making some Remarks on this scene. "Humph," says the boys, "this is nothing. The place is so Small we had not sea Room sufficient. If you had been with us on our big march you would have seen sights then." Well you see having Just Came into the sheepfold I am Green, yet but I'll soon get used to it no doubt. I say go to it boys give her Jesse. She richly Deserves it. She is the mother of Harlots. More anon.

---

[49] Ayers here again, as he does so many times, expresses his approval of the destruction of Southern property. He believed that South Carolina richly deserved destruction, particularly Charleston. Ayers himself seems to have been amazed at the efficiency of his comrades who had marched with Sherman "from Atlanta to the sea."

Still on The New[s] Jan. 25th 65.

Well I am going to tell you Something of how we are cituated here at the once Hardeeville for you reccollect I said in my former, this place had Disappeared, the Boys having it all Converted into Shantys and are now Living in them Like fighting fowls as they are for they Surely have proved themselves such on many hard fought Battlefields. Since we Came here it has been quiet Rainey and this being A low wet Country, makes it some disagreeable, tho for some two days past it has ceased Raining and we are doing fine now. This is A singular Country timbers all Evergreen makes it Look just like Spring or summer and then thare are frogs plenty here and they are singing Just as merily now as they do in the Spring season in Illinois or Indianna and seem Just as merry as Tho thare was no war in our Land and in fact our Boys Seem A little inspired in that way. They all seem Joyous and gleeful as tho they had not or had forgot that they have Just been wading through sees of blood. Well I Rejoice to see the Soaldiers in So fine Spirits. We have occasional meetings in the Regiments Especially on Sabbath and then we have organized into A Lyceum, Many of us in 129th and have our debates two and three Evening in Each week. This makes us fine passtime and here I must in Justice Say that I find that in my absence thare has been quiet a Change for the better. Thare is not near the Amount of Profanity and Low flung vulgarity and blaggardism that used to be used in our Reg. We are having brigade Drill this afternoon, the boys are all out on this Drill. So I find this Leisure moment. It is Rumered now that we are to have an Armistice of forty days and if so we Shall Stay here untill thats over. It Looks some Like Rain and is quiet Chilley. Last night was for this place quiet coald freesing ice quarter inch thick which has stoped the mouths of our neighbors the frogs. They are as Dum today as balims Coalt [*Balaam's ass*]. It seems as tho it is Rather hard for me to get Stout once more. I keep troubled with bowell Complaint sower Stomach and with my water so I cant Rest as I ought but feel greatful to my Maker it is as well as it is with me.   J. T. Ayers.

Well here once more Jan. 29eth 65.

This morning Drum beats at five and all hands on deck, once more having been previously warned the Evening before and Such Rumbling up and Tumbling up you can have no idea Except you was thare. We haistily got up and Et our grub and Packed up and all Ready for March at 7 O'clock A.M. We ware then formed into Line and Stacked Arms for half hour, and then the Boys pitched into Burning our fine Camps Chairs Stools Tables Bunks oald carts wheelbares and all and Every thing we had no use for. So Rolld out leaving this place to be Remembered among the things that was. The Third Division Laid here and Gen. Ward[50] Commands this Division so Away he goes and we after him for 18 miles and incamped for the night. Many of us pore soaldiers Laying down with weried Lims and Aching bones and in the morning Jan 30eth we moved again Eight miles further to A place Calld Robisonsville. Here we Halted for the present. Here we had A Small Skirmish with the Rebs. Here I Left the Army having completely give out the day before on the march and would have been Left had it not been for friend Quackenbush—Quartermaster Sargent of our Reg. I Rode his horse two miles in the evening was all saved my Bacon. Well here our Doctor sent me in Ambulance to Savanna River five miles to A place Called Sisterses ferry and here I took A boat for Savanna. Thare was quiet A number of us Came down that had gave out, two of them Dying on boat while Comeing, This Savanna River is Surely the Crookedest River I ever Saw,

---

[50] Brigadier General William Thomas Ward.

many places being so Short bends it was hard to Escape hitting Bank at some Point tho we Come through safe. This River has no banks on Either side but Spreads all over the bottoms on either Side, Lined all the way with thick growth of Pine palmetto and various other timbers all ever green. In fact all the timbers here are of the Evergreen, so you don't fully Realise that it is winter and in fact it aint winter for us Northerners but Just About proper heat to suit us tho Chilley and Disagreeable at night. It is hard to tell whare the army will Strike as Sherman keeps his own secrets—tho I Predict Charleston and then Richmon [*Richmond, Va.*]. He is getting his whole force in Line again 90 thousand Strong and can go Anywhare he Chooses in Dixie without hindrence. He has the finest Army in the world. South Carlina is doomed and the war nigh its close, sure no mistake in my mind. God Send how soon.

Feb 1st 65.

J.T. Ayers.

Not well by any means.

February 2nd 65. This is A Lovely morning, Just Like A morning in Aprile in Illinois. Nothing new as I know of this morning to Record. I feel some little better, still here in the Pavillion Hospital in west Part of Savanna and am fairing prety well.   J.T. Ayers.

3rd. It is Raining this morning some and is quiet Chilley and while I am writing this the Boys are hovering Round our Little fireplace, Some Smoking and Some talking. Thare is twelve of us Stored Away here in this tent. This Hospital is Sourrounded with A brick wall some 8 feet high and incloses About one Acre of ground. Thare is A Large Brick Building in here which Lines two sides of this intire Lot. I presume this has been A kind of a place for the Rich owner of those buildings to Rally his niggers morning and Evening by his overseer and task them and Call the Roll and no doubt But that many A nigger has been floged in this pen. I see in my travels many Similar places here in the South but those niger Pens are played out now thank God for that. Well this Citty of Savanna is or has been Rather Sightly for the South and Shows signs of having once possesst great wealth and perhaps will Again at some day, tho I Really think this whole South, or that part Called South Carlina with A large Portion of Georgia and Florida will be gave to the niggers for A possession. I Say give it to them. The Sourrounding Country Lyes verry Level, Soil Sandy and is mostly Covered with water from two inches to several feet. Here they Raise Rice by the thousand. They prepare there farms in this wise—they Cut Large Ditches or Canalls through there farms three or four of those Ditches being on one farm if Large. Generally there is A large big Canall Cut from the River out far in the Swamps and all those Smaller Ditches Lead at proper Angles into this Big Canall So by this process they keep the controle of those waters taking them off and letting them on at pleasure by having flood gates at Each end of those Ditches. Beside here is tide water so when the tide is up if they wish to water there Rice field they have only to open those flood gates and here Comes the water and then close those gates and Haold it so long as they wish to use it. Then when tide is down open those gates and the water all Runs off with the tide. They Raise the finest of Rice here and have made vast Sums of money here from the culture of this article. I must think this is A sickly place, the Country being so Low and Marsh. Well it is Rather hard to tell what Season of the [year] it is as the wether as A general thing is quiet mild and warm. All the timbers are of the Evergreen which gives nature at all seasons have A gay Appearance and ware it not for the fact of A sad Stillness in those forests, they being Deserted by the Common Native forest

Songsters. The Fethered tribe and Rebel women Seem to have in part Disappeared togeather. God send the women may never Return But you ye Little birds Yanks as we are we say to you Come back and bring with you those sweet notes, and Help us sing or you sing whilst we Listen to your sweet notes. Hail Collumbia you misst the Stars and Stripes did you, and those sweet notes had Died Away, in your Sunny Habitations. So you have been A long and tedious trip way North to catch the Sound once more. Your Little toes have all most frose while there in Exile. Come back now Little sweet songsters. You can see the stars and Stripes floating once more in your Native South and we Yanks will help you Sing the oald Heavenly sonet as in days of yore. Hail Collumbia Happy Land God help all Nature Join in the Song so mote it be.

J. T. Ayers.

Savanna Georgia Feb. 5th 65.

Well tho I am not well Still I find I am Some on the improve and as I have nothing Specially on hand only to attend at meal times and Devour Some Coffee and hard tack and Lounge Round between times I'll use some this Leisure in telling my friends Something more of the South. There are A great many Strange freaks in nature down here. Could one tell it all it Seems to me that he who was gifted in the Discriptive art and good at telling what he sees might write A Book that would be quiet interesting on the Manners, Customs, and habits of this People of the South, with A Description of the Country and its Surroundings. I have already toald you of her Rice fields and at what great Expence those Rice plantations are gotten up. I wish you to understand that Georgia and South Carlina grow Cotton on A Large Scale and of the finest quality. No Cotton can be produced that is better in quality I am told than the Sea Island Cotton which is Raised on those

Islands from Hilton head down the Coast as far as florida and then from what I See they Raise fine Corn and Sweet Potatoes and almost all kinds of Tropical fruits are Raised here in Abundance. And then they Scierce know when winter is on hand as the winters are verry mild. Now while I write Sitting in A Hospital tent it is so pleasant just like one of those finest of Aprile days in Illinois. And then the Scenery is grand and imposing in many ways. There is the Palmetto tree, tall Straight and beautiful Rearing her great green high head up Above her neighbors Sourrounding her making A noble Appearance to the beholder. And beside there is A kind of moss grows here on the Branches of the trees many of the Trees being hung full of this moss in some places all the timbers are Loaded or all there Branches. This moss Resembles in coller that of Water Rotted Hemp toe as you see it Where they have been breaking hemp and Switching it over the break as they do. You know thare is Strugleings [*stragglings*] fly off. Well this moss Looks Just as near as I can now Describe it Just Like those trees were gracefully hung full of this toe. This makes the forests have A novel, tho A beautiful appearance. Well I am toald there is great use made of this moss. It is geathered by the People and used for matrasses under beds, Stuffing sofas &c., being verry useful. This moss makes the most beautiful Display and Appearance when growing on those Live oak trees, which grow numerous here. Those Live oaks are Shaped similar to the Apple tree only they grow quiet Larg Spreading there Lims far Around. They Don't grow high nor more than from 8 to 12 feet untill they Branch out Just like the Apple tree. Many of those trees hang full of this moss and they being evergreen makes the sight most Lovely——

Here I Resume Again—Feb. 6th 65, it Raining this morning A little and is quiet Chilly. I am Still mending Slowly,

Rested well Last night. Just been to breakfast, had Coffee hard tack and small piece of Coald boiled Beef. We have A big fire in Some Large Buildings Acrost the Street oposite us. Several ingines are at work and A large crowd gathered Round as Spectators, but in the midst of the flames quiet a Cannonading Broke Loose, one of those buildings being stored with Loaded guns. They commenced playing A merry tune and you had better see the Crowd Scatter. From present appearance they will quash the fire from Spreading any further. It happens to be a favourable time as the wind don't Blow much and Raining as it is A little. There is A Large Arsenal near by this fire. Had it of Reached that we would seen fun. Thare was A fire here A few days since which Burst out in one of those Arsenals and made an Awful Splash Roaring and Cannonading at A fearful Rate killing and wounding many that was Round in its Presincts and producing great terror to all. A vast Amount of Shells bursted Scattering there fragments all Round to the great danger of all. It is said to be done by the Rebs. I have no doubt of this and had I my way, the next time they fired this Cursed whole, Ide moove all the Gov. property outside   take all the troops and Set the place all in flames and let it go to the Devil whare it belongs. Well I am not prepared now to tell you much of the manners and Customs of this People as I have had no Chance to Learn being as I have Shut up in this Hospital and no getting out only with A pass and Seldom you Can get that. Just now the firemen are Passing by here singing one of there fire Songs. It Sounds well to me as I sit here. The firemen here are all darkies and when they fight and Conquer A big fire Like the one Just on hand they feel well and will Express there feelings by singing and you know they sing Harty. Well I must stop now and Rest. I'll come back Again Soon.   J. T. Ayers.

Well Here I come Feb. 7th 65.

I Left Savanna yesterday at one O'clock P.M. on Steamer for Hilton Head in Company with 200 Convallesence from the Several Hospitals that was there. We are all ordered back to our Regiments. We had A merry Ride Again on oald Ocean. The oald thing seems to be mad always or at Least when I get on her Lap she gets the figets teribly and tosses herself from side to side thinking posably she can throw us off of her Lap, but we Stuck her and made her Carry us, tho she plunged and frisked at such A Rate the Boys all got Sick and tryed to heave the oald thing from there Stomachs and they made prety fair efforts in that way. But oald mamma was Still on hand Rocking Away. Well we Landed here About ½ past 7 this Morning. It Rained all night and is Still Raining Some which makes it quiet disagreeable. We ware marched from warf to marshalls office. Here our Roll was Calld, then after Some delay marched up in Town to an oald warehouse and here we have quarters for the present. We have Just made a little Coffee and Eat our meal and now feel fine for Soaldiers. Here I fell in with the orderly of Co. E, Mr. Olney; he is gon now to Savanna. This Hilton Head is Rather Handsome beside quiet A place. Here I see some the Largest Cannon I ever saw. They are as Large as the trunks of great trees and A numerous Supply of them at that and Shell piled up in great abundance, as big Round as the head of A flower barrel. Well when we move I'll tell you. I am feeling prety well this morning. Oald Mamma Cant make me york and oop as She does the Boys. I am too oald for her. I'll come Again—Feb. 7th 65—J.T.A.

Cheers Cheers for our heroes
Not those who ware Stares
Not those who ware Eagles
And Leaffets and bars
We know they are gallant
And honor them two
For bravely maintaining
The Red white and Blue

But Cheers for our Soldiers
Rough Rinkled and brown
The men who makes heroes
And ask no Renown
Unselfish untiring
Interpid and true
The bulwark Sourrounding
The Red white and blue

Our Patriot Soldiers
When Treason Arose
And Freedoms own Children
Assaild he as foes
When Anarchy assailed
And order withdrew
They Rallyed to Rescue
The Red white and blue

Uphoalding our banner
On many A field
The doom of the Traitor
They valiantly sealed
And worn with thes conflicts
Found vigor Annew
Where victory greeted
The Red white and Blue

Yet Loved ones have fallen
And Still where they Sleep
A Sorrowing nation
Shall Silently weep
And Springs fairest flowers
In gratitude Strew
Ore those who have Cherished
The Red white and Blue

But Glory immortal
Is waiting them now
And Chaplets unfading
Shall bind Every Brow
When Calld by the trumpet
At times great Review
They Stand who Defended
The Red white and Blue

Jas. T. Ayers,[51] Feb. 7th 65
At Hilton Head South Carlina
It is on the Bank of Mother Ocean

At Blairs Landing South Carolina
60 miles Above Hilton Head, Sunday evening Feb. 12th 65.
Came here friday evening. We are incamped all over the Land, Some 5 thousand of us convallascence formed into Battallions, 14th 15th 17th and 20eth Army Corpse are all Represented here and are in Seperate battallions. And I was yestarday Detailed Postmaster of the whole. We are having beautiful wether here now Just Like Spring. The Rumer is the Rebs are fleeing from Charleston and Sherman has taken the Citty[52] and Rumer says Peace is made.[53] This I dont believe. Well I am doing Prety well now, health Some on the improve. I have A tent all alone close by Col. tent at Headquarters. J.T. Ayer.

Still at Blairs Landing Feb. 14th 65.
All seems to be going on fine. It is Raining Slowly this forenoon. No Special news yet from Sherman. Rumer tho is Cheering all Round. J.T. A.

Feb. 15th 65—Still here at Blairs Landing on Pocatalico River South Carlina. It Rained all afternoon and night, has Clered

---

[51] These verses appear at this point in Ayers' diary. It should be noted that Ayers signed as well as dated practically every entry. Thus Ayers' signature below these verses does not necessarily indicate a claim to authorship. Frequently he stated that he had copied the verses from a newspaper. There can be no doubt that the first verse expresses Ayers' attitude toward commissioned officers.
[52] The Union forces occupied Charleston on February 18, 1865.
[53] Ayers perhaps referred to the efforts, February 3, 1865, of the Union and Confederate commissioners to agree on peace terms at the Hampton Roads Conference.

off now warm and fine. News Came here Last evening that A large boddy of Rebs were Close on us and the Steam Boat General Hooker had just Arived with arms and Accouterments for us all. So the officers has been busy arming the Companyes and batallions all night and are Still busy arming. We all being mostly convallascencts we had no guns. We are prety well Armed now for the Jonneys So Just let them Come. Well I am Satisfyed of one thing that in Proportion to our numbers here we have more thieves and Robbers than any other crowd. It beats all how they steal and that from one another and even Rob one another. We have in this Camp the off Scourings of all Gods Creation. I thought I was wide Awak for them but they are two Smart for me. Today one of those Scamps came in my tent to trade for my Revolver and while here before my eyes Stole my Powder flask and got Away safe. These Bounty Jumpers and Convallacences Can beat the Devil Sure and certain. I'll Come back Again soon.   J. T. Ayers.

Southcarolina Feb. 16th 65. Still here. Fine beautiful morning, All Astir. Some are Leaving on Boat for Pocatalico Bridge Above here wither we will soon all go I Suppose. I dont feel So well this morning. Had pore Rest Last night. My water troubles me so. Nothing new this morning. J.T. Ayers.

Saturday Feb. 18th 1865. Combihee River or Landing Haywood Plantation SouthCarolina.

This is A Lovely morning Spring Like. We Landed here yestarday Evening, Having left Blairs Landing on Pocatalico River Evening before. We Came by Boat by way of Beaufort and after traveling some 200 miles by water we are only 12 miles from whare we Started from—Blairs Landing. This is the most Sightly Place I have yet Saw in Southcarolina, Say two thirds of as far as one Can See open and balance, handsomely doted over with groves of Live oak and Pine timbers and the Country Lyes high and Beautifully Roaling and from the appearance of the Soil is Ritch and good. Close by us on our South I see A Larg Plantation and fine looking Buildings, I am toald there is two negro Regiments and one white Reg. Camped here beside ours which makes A pretty fair force here. We are Just getting Ready now to Stretch our tents. I'll come Again soon.   J.T. Ayers.

At Charleston Southcarlina, Thursday Evening Feb. 23rd 1865.

Well we Received marching orders Monday forenoon 20eth Feb and we Struck tents in less than no time and away we go taking the main Road from here or Rather from Savanna and marched all the way through 60 miles. Part of our Road was quiet good and part Desperately bad so we had to work our way on as best we Could. The day we left Camp the Ajutant Presst A Span of mules and waggon and we Piled on the trunks Carpet Sacks Camp cittles and dinner Boxes. This was A great assistance tho we had hard work to get through those mud holds, but when the waggon would Mire in Mud we would Rush in and Lay hold of the waggon and push her out. We had fine wether all the way, and mostly all the Rout Level and Low. Some few places was Rather inticing, but mostly all the Rout was A Low swampy Country full of Alligaters the niggers says. Thare was many A pore Chicken Duck goose and turkey Departed this Life on our march. Sweet potatoes and Honey not much to be had but the Boys got what was on hand. Most all the Buildings and Bridges we Burned as we marched and the Country for some distance on Either side of Road is Laid A moral waste. Well here we are sure and Certain on A Little Rising ground write in full view of the Critter[54] only the River betwean it and us. She

---

[54] Charleston, S. C. Ayers further expresses his feelings about Charleston and South Carolina and his hopes for their punishment on p. 88.

makes A fine Appearance at this distance. I am toald the
Rebel troops all Evacuated the Citty and our forces marched
in and have full Possession. Hurrau for the union. Ritchmon
[*Richmond, Va.*] comes down next and then where is Rebellion, why Blowed up. I'll tell more next time.   J.T.A.

Charleston S. C. Feb. 26th 65.

It Rained yesterday mostly all day and Some Little During Last night, is Cloudy this morning and quiet warm and
pleasant. Some blossoms have made there appearance and
vegitation is Springing up here now Rapidly. We had A
funeral yesterday in Camp. One of our Soldiers Died night
before. He appeared to be A Stranger Amongst us all tho I
Lerned he was from Philadelphia. Our Battalion Some two
thousand in number is made up of men from 14th 17th 15th
and 20eth Corpse and therefore are mostly Strangers to one
another. We are now A convallascent Corpse. The Commander Came to me yesterday and inquired if I was not A
Preacher. I answered in the Afirmative. He then wished me
to manage the funeral which I did as best I could. After the
Pore Soaldier was Lowered in his grave having no Coffin or
Box to Lay him in we wrapped him up in his Blanket and
Layed him down to Rest till Awaked by Gabriels Trump. I
made Some Remarks then sung "and must I be to Judgment
brought," prayed with the Soldiers and we Piled the Earth
upon the Earth and Left our Strange Brother Soldier to take
his Rest far here in the South. God bless his Friends and Con-
sole his widow and orphant Children. Yesterday and this
morning I am not as well as I could wish. I feel Stupid sore
and half used up tho I keep a good Appetite thank God and
here I must Say we do and Can get plenty of oisters and I have
become verry fond of them. Can sit down Crack and fill A
pint cup of them   Sprinkle A little Pepper and Salt with A
little vinega on them then   take A Spoon and pitch into

them with A good Relish and Surely with a good Grace. You would Laughf to see me at those oisters. I Can Demolish A quart of them at A time. We are only getting About half Rations now but I understand tomorrow we will Draw full Rations and tho when we came here Charleston was A Deserted Citty it is filling up Rapidly and in A few days will Present A Business Appearance Again as General Hatch[55] has ordered business to Resume. Charleston is A Large Citty and has A fine Appearance—Balance when I Come Again—

                                                      J.T. Ayers.

Well here I am Again—March 9th 65 and Still at Charleston.

We have been having A Rainey time for several days past, wether warm and pleasant. Timbers are Leaveing out grass growing fine. Birds are Singing merily. All nature Sems Joyous here now and ware it not for the desolation this Cruel war has made in these parts this would be Rather A Desire place. But the war has Completely Destroyed this once Beautiful Citty and Country all Round. In fact SouthCarolina is and Soon will be Laid in Ruins by fire and Sword and when we Remember that this State was first to susceed and Rebell and that here at Charleston Rebellion was plotted and Hatched, and that write here Stands fort Sumpter whare the Rebs fired there first gun who Can pitty. True thare are some good Union People here in Charleston but they are Rather Scierce. Well I have been attending A protracted Meeting at Bethel Church held by the Darkies. I was there afternoon and at night on Sunday and attended Monday and Tuesday nights and invited Seekers forward for prayers and on Each night Some forty Came forward. Last night I did not attend as I was tired and needed Rest. I am Doing well here and feel wel and So I'll Close now.   J.T. Ayers.

[55] John Porter Hatch. On February 26 he was given command of the Charleston District, Department of South Carolina.

March 17th 65.   Still here at Charleston S. C.
The wether is fine now.   Spring is here in all her Glory. Everything seems Joyous and gleeful. We are greatly Rejoiced at the tidings to day of the overthrow of Ritchmon[56] and other Cheering news.   It begins to Look something like this cruel war was nigh over.   Hope it may be so.   My health now is fine and am doing well.   J.T. Ayers.

March 20eth 65 Monday morning and still at Charleston
It is Clear beautiful and warm this morning.   Nothing new Astir.   We had A glorious good meeting Last night in the 14th Corpse.   Many from 20eth Corpse and Cavalry Corpse Came over.   I spoke for A short time from thease words: "And while he was yet A great way off his Father saw him and Ran and fell on his neck imbraced and kisst his son." The subject was a good one and had A powerful affect.   Many felt the power of God Last night and felt to promise to do better.   God bless the Effort and Convert the Boys is my prayer for Jesus Sake.   J.T.A.

March 28th 65 and Still at Charleston.
Well it has been Raining all day and is Rather Disagreeable.   Our news is quiet good, prospects fair for Closing this Cruel war soon.   We are having prety fair times here now. Plenty to eat health find and all joyful.   We are having some interesting prayer meetings of evenings.   We hoald these meeting thre and four evenings through the week.   On Last Sundy evening some 20 or more Came forward for prayers as seekers.   God bless the Boys and Most Gloriously Revive his work in our midst.   Oh how I wish I was more gifted and had more grace so I might be more useful.   Lord give me wisdom.   I hope soon to get news from home.   Have had none since I left.   J.T. Ayers.

---

[56] Richmond did not fall until April 3; the news of its "overthrow" on March 17 was premature.

WROTE[57] AT CHARLESTON S.C. MARCH 29TH 65
BY J.T. AYERS

1st   Sinners perhaps this news with you
       May have no weight altho tis true
       The Carnel pleasures of the Earth
       Cast off the thoughts and fears of Death

2nd   The aged Sinner will not turn
       His hart so hard he cannot mourn
       Yay harder than the flinty Rock
       That will not break tho Jesus knock

3rd   The Blooming youth all in his prime
       Is Counting up his Length of time
       He oft times says tis his intent
       When he gets oald he will Repent

4th   But oh the sad and awful State
       Of those who Stay and Come two Late
       The foolish Virgins did begin
       To knock but Could not enter in.

5   When Christ the Lord shall come Again
       In Solem pomp and burning flame
       Saying Gabriel go proclaim the sound
       Awake ye nations under ground

6th   Oh how will parents tremble thare
       Whove Raised there Children without prayer
       Me thinks I hear the Children say
       We never herd our parents pray

7th   Then parents take A solem view
       Of your Dear Children near to you
       How Can you bare to hear them cry
       And Charge you with there Miserry.

8th   Good Lord what groans what bitter cryes
       What Rumbling thunders throug the skyes
       Pore sinners sinking in Dispair
       And Christians Shouting through the air

---

[57] "Wrote" may mean either composed or copied by J. T. Ayers. See note 51.

(I feel well this morning.[58]
I was waid yesterday, 168 Lbs
being in 2 Lbs of as heavy
as ever I waid.)

9th   Oh Glorious day oh blessed hope
My soul Leaps forward at the thought
That in Heavenly happy throng
I'll meet my friends before me gon.

10th   With wings that will outshine the goald
What Happiness will thare unfold
When I with friends begin to meet
Our happiness will be Complete.

At Charleston S. C. Apr. 8th 65

Well we are Still here in this Cruel mean Secesh Citty and ar having Some warm wether, timbers all out in full Leaf, Peaches as big as quails Eggs and the figs ar Large as common sised Crabapples and fig trees are plenty here and loaded this year. This is no place for apples nor for tame grass. The Land is two Sandy and Climate two hot for it to prosper. This Country brings fine Corn of the york kind, Sweet potatoes mellons Ry and &c grow prety well and Rice and Cotton grow fine. Most of the Country Round here is Low and Marshey and thickly set with Pine timber. Thare is some Live oak and then thare is here as I have before Described down in Georgia plenty of this moss hanging on the timbers Round here. In fact this is A Novel Country taking it all in all. Even the People are A kind of quare creature allmost as Ignorant as the negro and in many Casses more so. Charleston is an unsightly place, no taste, all oald fashioned and fifty years behind the times, Streets filthy and the whole place stinks so as to make it unpleasant to walk The Streets, tho this may ware Away after Secession is wiped out of the place. Tho I fear we shall not

---

[58] Ayers may have been interrupted while he was copying or composing, or may just have felt moved to note that he, too, was improving in health.

improve there morals very much, for most assuredly we have Some Scalawags in our Ranks as mean and Devlish as Satan wants them to be. In fact sometimes they make the Devil blush. Many of our Boys will push into houses where only women are the inmates and Steal and Rob all the Can Lay there unholy hands on and often treat the women Rudely, beside tareing up womens Dresses Bonnets and so on. Well thease trifleling pukes are A disgrace to the great union Army and are found mostly Among those Substitutes and thousand doler men. For an Example of there utter Recklessness we ware Hoalding Evening meetings and I prevailed on A man with A team to go with me and one or two others out some distance and get a Load of Joice and Plank from an oald waist place for seets to accommodate our meeting and these Demons Came and Stold the Last plank and Joist Away, A thing I could not believe men Could be found mean Enoughf to Do. Such men aint fit for Dog feed. 　　　　　J.T.Ayers

Charleston, S.C., Apr 12th 65.

Well I am Still here and well thank God. You see Above that the Scamps of 20eth Corpse Stold our seats we had provided for meeting but this I think has had A good affect. Instead of producing A damper on our Efforts it has caused A greater Exertion on our part and many attend now feeling an indignity for the mean act and we are having glorious good meetings. Over 20 came forward for prayers night before Last and Last night perhaps 30 or more and we are having precious times. Lord work for thy names Glory and our good. It is prety hard on me as I have to Lead and manage all those Meetings. Well we are all injoying good health now. Boys all in best of spirits at the good news of A prospect of an end to this war soon. The Boys of my mess have been out and Brought in one of those hand mills and set it up in the Rear

of our Buglesmans tent and mine and we grind Corn and have
the finest of Corn Cakes and fried much now Laying Mr. Hard
tack quiet in the Shade. The Boys are grinding away now
while I write this. They have Contifistticated A Sausiage
Cutter and we have Just been Drawing some nice Lean toughf
beef but the Boys Stick this beef in the Cutter and Chaw it all
up so you see we can get at it, then. The wether is verry fine
now tho prety warm. Well we are Looking for A big time
friday at Sumpter in Raising our flag; thare will be A Jolly
big Crowd here then. Jas. T. Ayers.

Apr 15th 65. Well the 14th has past and truly A memerable
day will it be for all time to Come. The vast Crowd in attendance, the Beautiful Display of Collers and flags from The
Steamers and Shiping and Scooners was Grand beyond Discription. Far Away all Round Sumpter was thick as A forest
of trees was those vessels brought up in Battle Aray. And
then on Morris Island and forts moltrie [vacant space] they
two was Decorated and flags high up in the air flying and all
Alive with human beings and then the vast crowds of men
women and Children on the Islands as Spectators to witness
this grand event. There was A grand view of the whole proceedings from Charleston from James Island and St. Andrews
Island and those places of observation was Alive with Human
soals all in brethless silence waiting the opening of the great
Ball which was to take Place at 12 o'clock but from Some
Cause did not Commence untill ten minutes after one P.M.
Then Sumpter Raised the flag and Boom went A gun from
Fort Moltrie at Sumter. This opened the Ball and Sumpter
the vessels the forts and Batterrys all pitched in peal after
peal untill the earth trembled. It was Arranged that it was A
Sham battle. All the Different forts and Batterrys and ves-
sels ingaged Against Sumpter. I tell you, Sumpter made

things howl. I could see the fire Role from her great guns Like great flashes of lightning taking the whole senery as it accurred. It Surely was grand. I selected for my observatory a Large tree that stands near my tent. Climeing high up in this tree I had A fine view of the whole senerry and to add to the grandure of the occasion there was two hundred guns fired on the official news of Lees surrender.[59] Oh but we Soaldiers ware Joyous over this glorious news. Early in the morning A news Boy Came Round in Camp hollowing "here's your papers." We bought one and Commenced Reading thus: "General Lee has Surrendered his intire force up to General Grant, signed E.M. Stanton." We Raised the yell and I and Sargent Majer Piled our hats in the fire and burned them having said previously we would do So when Lee Surrendered. And we all began to be merry as the family did when the Prodigal Came home. All we failed in was the fated Calf but we had good hard tack, sowbelly and hot coffee for breakfast and with glad Harts this was perhaps as Joyous A time as the occasion the Saviour Speaks of. So all is waggin on fine and Peace will and must soon follow and we all permited soon to Return home God send how soon. My health is good thank God for his mercy.   Jas. T. Ayers.

Moorehead Citty N.C. Apr 18th A.D. 1865.

Just Landed here. Came from Charleston, S.C. by way of Wilmington N.C. on Steamer Champion. Left Charleston on Sunday Apr. 16th. Have had a pleasant trip wether fine, boat Roomey and Comfortable, no accidents nor Deaths on trip, but we meet the Sad news here of the assassination of President Lincon[60] which Saddens my Hart. God have mercy on us. What is there man wont do. I fear we are all bound for

---

[59] At Appomattox Court House, Virginia, April 9, 1865; the formal surrender was made on April 12. President Lincoln designated April 14, the fourth anniversary of the firing upon Fort Sumter, for the formal raising of the United States flag over its ruins.
[60] Lincoln was shot on the night of April 14 and died the next morning.

the Devil Head long. I hope we Shant Stay here long as this is A little unsightly place tho A vast amount of Ships and Scooners are laying here and at Beaufort in sight of this place. Wilmington is Rather Small to what I was looking for. I'll Come soon Again.   J.T. Ayers.

Moorehead Citty N.C. Apr 19th 1865.

As I Stated on the other Side we Came here yestarday from Charleston S.C. from which place we Started Sunday morning Apr 16th by way of Wilmington N.C. and marched out south of Town one and ½ miles and pitched tents ar Rather Camped for the night and we was not here but A Short time untill we ware ordered to be Ready for marching by six this morning for Newbern 36 miles from here. And when time Came we only had two waggons furnished to Hall all our Bagage so all officers plunder was left to go by Rail this afternoon at 4 o'clock and I with A few others are detailed to gard and Superintend this Bagage through. Boys all Rolld out at 8 o'clock and here am I. This is A beatiful day after Raining all night and Ducking many of nicely as we had not put up our tents as we Should of done.   J.T. Ayers.

Thursday morning At Newbern N.C. Apr 20eth 1865.

Came here yestarday Evening by Car train. Camped over night in Carell [corral] Spread down my gun and pup tent and knapsack for Pillow. Spread my Blanket over me on top of sand pile and had A good nights Rest. This morning Perry Stephens, Jesse Sphinks and myself have joined Pups and Stretched her up out on Street close by this Carell and here we are waiting for the Boys to Come up who are marching through from Moorehead Citty here. They will Reach here tomorrow if no accident takes place. I Read Last evening A Dispatch from Sherman, Stoping Hostilitys[61] and A prospect

---

[61] Sherman and Joseph E. Johnston agreed upon terms on April 18. The Confederate surrender occurred on April 26.

of Speedy peace and A Return of the Soldiers Home and ware it not for the Sad news of the Assasination of President Lincon we Should all Shout for Joy. But alass all our Joy is turned into mourning at the Sad news. Never was there A baser act Commited and never did a pureer patriot fall in Defence of his Country than President Lincon. God will Avenge his Blood on the transgressors. It is Just Commencing to Rain and bids fair for A Rainey time. As we Came A Long yesterday I had the pleasure of seeing one of those Customers Calld Aligaters. It was say Six feet Long and he that Looks at the Picture in Websters Spelling Book[62] has there shape prety Correctly. So far as I have saw of N.C. it is low and marshy thick set all over with Pine timber and verry Sandy and I am of opinion pore. I noticed at Bufort [*Beaufort*] and at Moorehead Citty as well as here all the Shiping and vessels with colers half Mast in Consequence of the Sad news of the murder of the President. Jas. T. Ayers. I'll come again soon.

Coppy from Left Page   [*Left page contained same information in rough-pencil*]

Raleigh N.C.	Apr 27th 65.	
Thos. Shaw Dr.	2.00	
J. D. Rilea Dr.	5.25	("for overcoat")
John Selmon	2.00	
Asaac Vail	1.50	
L. C. Tracy	1.00	
S. A. Cables	1.00	
Sage	1.25	
Gilmon for watch	16.00	
	30.00	
May 12th D. Acker Dr. Cash	59.85	
	89.85	

---

[62] The reader may wonder what Ayers sought in Webster's Spelling Book. The pictures seem to have impressed him.

Do by cash
Do for clothing   6.50
Borrowed and for coat $6.00
and one shirt— $1.00
Hains   8.35
Zentner   3.50
Co. D. man   2.00
Englet   25.00
Lt. Chiteul, note.   21.00
_____
Sargent   59.85
B. A. Barber
Dr. cash $1.50
all Left with Lt. Fitch of Co. E for collection.
Lt. Chiteul Dr. for p[l]ug tobacco 1.00
The above set below thus—   89.85
_____
90.85
John Smith Cash $1.50
The above Amount is Due me and Left with Lieut B. F. Fitch for Collection, of Co. E 129th Reg. Ills vol inft.

Jas. T. Ayers May first 65 and at
Newbern N.C.
Fine day verry Pleasant.

At Raleigh N.C. Apr 28th 65.

My health this morning is good tho some tired after my Big walk yesterday. We was marched from here on Tuesday 15 miles on the Holly Spring Road and Camped and here we Staid untill Johnson[63] surrendered and at two O'clock P.M. yestarday we Pulld up and Came back to Raleigh and here we are Joyous at the Glorious news of Peace and hopes of home once more. Raleigh is Rather Beautiful, the Country Round is Rolling and verry Stoney.   J.T. Ayers.

Sunday morning at Newbern N.C. Apr 30eth A.D. 1865.

Well I am here this morning. Came here yesterday at noon from Raleigh. My health is quiet good thank God and

_____

[63] Johnston's surrender (see note 61) marked the end of effective organized resistance in the South.

best of all is this Cruel war is over and I trust A permanent
Peace is made. Having knocked the nigger out of thos ungodly Traitors and taught them A Lesson they nor there Children nor there Childrens Children will never forget that being
Southerners dont necessarily make them better than other men
and there fighting qualities far superior to Any other People,
But that, Man to man, they can only fight as best they Can Like
others. I feel they will be quiet now, and we shall be able
once more to Live with them in Peace, the great Cause of all
this great war being Removed, Slaverry. Never do I trust in
God will Slaverry be Sanctioned in this goverment Again.
Peace Oh what Joyful news is this to us pore Soldiers. No
Set of men in all Gods Creation has A write to Rejoice and
Even Shout over the glad tidings of Peace more than the war
worne Veteran. He who has with Musket and bayonet
Waded throug Snow, Rain, Hail, and Swamp, Amidst Rivers
of Blood Living on Hard tack and Sowbelly with the Heavens
for our dwelling place for the Space of four Long years far
from our Homes and friends in the midst of Enemys Boath
Male and female. Why should we not Rejoice at Peace and
A Return to our Beautiful Homes and warm Harted friends
far in the North. My Hart Leaps for Joy while I write but
Alass whare is our Great Leader President Lincon. He has
been Stricken down by the fowl Hand of an Assassion Just at
A time when he and the Nation was About to Reap the Re-
ward of his and there Labours and he be permited to injoy
A season of Rest from his Labours. We Shall never see his
Smiling face no[r] her his powerful voice nor be instructed by
his wise Counsel while in this flesh Again. In the assassination and Death of Abraham Lincon Ilinois Has Lost her
noblest and brightest son. But Believeing as I do that he was
A Christian and tho in him we have Lost A great wise and
good Leader we are the Looseers while he is the gainer, being

far better off than we who Remain. And I trust God will over Rule the Sad Affair to the Good of the Nation. It makes my Hart bleed to see Towns Cittys Shipping and men all Draped in mourning and Reflect that A Nations Pride has been by the foul hand of A Ruffian Stricken from our midst. May God bless our incomeing President, indue him with wisdom and Let A double portion of Father Abrahams Spirit Rest on him and help him guide the Ship of State Safe to Honor and to Glory, So mote it be.   Jas. T. Ayers.

Friday May 5th 1865. We have Just Left Newbern N.C. some 9 hundred for Home. We are Aboard of two Small Scooners Propelld by two Small Steamers. Our Scooners are Lashed to each other side by side and follow in the Rear of the propellers. On yesterday afternoon at five O'clock Mr. Harkless Died in Newbern. He Lived at Ellisville Fulton Co., Ills. His wifes Name Maryann Harkless. This fine pleasant afternoon and in high glee.   J.T. Ayers.

Saturday 10 A.M. We are just Drawing Rations now. I Rose up and Looked all Round and nothing to be Seen but A wide world of Water and the two Little Steamers side by side Lashed fast to Each other puffing Away and our two oald Barges or Canall boats in Rear fastened by tow Ropes to those Steamers. We two are Lashed fast to each other side by side. This is A Lovely morning, ocean Calm and Smooth. My health never better than now. May 6th 1865. J. T. Ayers. Was in Pamlico Sound yestarday.

Hour by son in Evening passing by Rhoanoke Island.[64] Leaving it on our Left. Thare is A Small Citty here. Day has

---

[64] Ayers is describing the voyage from Newbern, N. C., down the Neuse River into Pamlico Sound, thence past Roanoke Island into Albemarle Sound to Elizabeth City and through the Dismal Swamp Canal to Norfolk, Virginia, on Chesapeake Bay, and thence up the Potomac River. This inside route avoided the dangers of storms off Cape Hatteras and permitted the use of the smaller steamers.

been beautiful and pleasant. Every thing went off fine. Once and A while we see A great sea fish.   J.T. Ayers.

Sunday Morning May 7th 65. Fine prety morning. Wind blows some, sea tossing, Boat Rolling, so you see I can hardly write. We are now in Albamarl Sound. Our two Little Steamers are puffing and pulling Away at us on our Boats.   J.T. Ayers.

We are now on the Rhoanoke Canall ½ Eleven o'clock A.M.
We came into this canall from broad River.—Passt through Canall out into Pauluset Sound 12 miles and then into Dismal Swamp River. We are here in this River at 6 p.m. and then passt into Albermarl Canall or as I would call it Dismal Swamp Canall and here we are in this canall this morning at Sunrise May 8th 65. This is a perfect swamp sure and certain. We Traveled yestarday for some time on Elizabeth River—

Well Here we are at Norfolk, Virginia Laying at Warf May 8th at 20 minutes to Eleven A.M. We have had A pleasant trip from Newbern N.C. here. Wether fine   ocean Calm, Rivers and Canalls all full of seneerry and Curiosity Even to Snakes, tho Amidst all we have been grossly imposed on in the Line of Rations, not getting half Enoughf.   J.T.A.

Well we Left Norfolk yestarday May 9th 65 at ½ past 4 P.m. for Elexander [*Alexandria, Va.*] We passt over Chesepeak Bay. It was quiet Roughf as it Rained and blew quiet A gail Just as we were Leaving Norfolk. We are now far up the Potomach and she is as Smooth as A fair maden is just before A big wedding, and our steamer sneasing and Puffing on A merry Rate at some ten miles per hour this ½ past 10 A.M. May 10th 65. We Shall soon be at Elexander our place of Destination. It is Coudy and some cool this forenoon.
    Jas. T. Ayers.

Well here we are at Elexander at 5 P. m. May 11th, 65, and some ten or 12 thousand incamped all Round west of the Citty in full sight Close by subburbs and all in high glee at the Joyous tidings of home and friends. May 11th 65. J.T. Ayers.

Well Still here at Elexandria Va. May 15th 65. Have Just been taking A walk. We are tented Round here west of the Citty and Amediately Ajoining as far as Eye can See on Either side of Rail Road Leading from here to Ritchmon. I suppose that thare is now over 50 thousand tented here and in a day or two we Shall have 150 thousand as Sherman[65] will be here with his entire Army tomorrow or next day and then we feel in hopse of Soon starting for Ills. The wether now is fine and best of All is we have Caught Jef Davis[66] and his intire Staff and now I hope he will hang and as he was Caught in womens Close I hope he will be Honored with A womans Suit to hang in—pore Coward puppy, two mean to Live, two mean to Dy—A man Starver, A soal killer, A dastard Rascal, A midnight assassion, A thief, A Rober, A Liar, A forsworn vilian, A Confirmed Traitor, A Slave Driver, A nigger breeder, A negro Equality man mixing his own Blood with niggers. He ought to hang. He has made fatherless Children by tens of thousands and widows by thousands has Caused the Spilling of Rivers of Blood. Hang him I say in A suit of some one of his Negro womens Close and Leave him on the Gallows for Crows and vultures to feed on. Make him an Example so as to deter others. My health is good.   J. T. Ayers.

Well here I sit before my tent dore three miles East of Washington City near the R. R. Leading from Washington Cty to Baltimore Cty and near by the East Branch of the Poto-

---

[65] The Grand Review of the Armies was held on May 24. The troops were encamped in and around Washington for days.

[66] Davis was captured at Irwinville, Ga., on May 10, while trying to escape from the country.

mach Saturday afternoon. We have A Lovely Place for camping being handsomely covered over with yong Pine timber and handsomely Rolling. We have Just finished Clearing Trimming and sweeping our Camp off and it Looks fine now. We have prety fair water, and I feel that we have A good healthy Location here and then the Health of our Reg is good, and we are fairing well in the Line of Rations. Beside the saniterry[67] is visiting us occasionally with A few of the Luxuryes of Life such as potatoes onions Pickels Dried fruit paper ink and etc. All we Lack is A Little money, yes A Little money to bless ourselves with and then all would be well. Our officers are making out our pay rolls today and we shall soon have A Little money. Well Hurraugh for the money. I presume we shall soon be started homewards and then wont we be Joyous. How fathers harts will Leap at the idea of having the pleasure once more of meeting there Pratling Children, Husbands meeting there wives, friends once more imbracing Each other. Happy day. God bless the soldiers, give them A happy pasport home and A Joyful meeting with friends. May 24th 65.

---

[67] The reference is to the United States Sanitary Commission's activities in the camps.

APPENDIX I

[This appendix contains poems and bits of verse which were written in the diary in Ayers' handwriting. Some of them he copied from newspapers, and some are obviously his own compositions. Among them are a few diary entries for the fall of 1863—the year Ayers recruited under the Johnson plan. The diary proper started Dec. 25, 1863.]

A SONG MADE AND WRITTEN BY J. T. AYERS, APR 1st, 1863.

Tune Cheer Up My Lively Lads

1st South Tunnel[1] here in Tennessee
Is as Strang A place as one Might see
Its up and down and down and up
From Deep Ravines to Mountain Top.

2nd The Rail Road Tunnel you must know
It passes throug those Mountains here
And if in Center you should be
Its dark as Midnight Certainly

5th The tunnels here they number two
From South to North as you pass through
Our Gards they Stand at Either end
The Rail Road Trains for to defend

6th The Hills are Spread here all Around
In Multitude they do Abound
The Sight most Lovely here I see
Is this Big Hill on which we be

7th From this high Hill it may be seen
Down South of us Sweet field of Green
And to behold it Looks so fine
Your Hart for it would Almost pin

8th If all the people here was Write
And Rebelism used up quiet
The Last infernal tory shot
And all the Torys Brought to naught

---

[1] South Tunnel is a town in Sumner County, northeast of Nashville.

9th   This place then would be paradise
All nature seems in place so nice
The Country fine as need to be
The health they say is Tolerably.

10th   And now the Grass is Growing fine
The leaves are Comeing fourth on vine
Some trees begin to Look quiet Green
And Leaves are plenty to be seen.

This is ninth verse
Fine weather now while this I write
Altho it was quiet Coald Last night
This Aprile first in sixty three
And here I'll end my Poetry.

10th   This days so fine and pleasant two
I hardly know how I should do
I said Above Ide End my Rhyme
I thought I had Just Closed in time.

11th   But here Again I'll use my pen
At Length more fully to Explain
This Country tho so fine it be
Is not the Country now for me.

12th   I love that Country thats all free
In this mankind should all Agree
Altho some men may have black skin
God himself has made them men.

13th   And while I do believe in God
And in my Hart trust in his word
The time has Come besure at last
That God will free the whole Black Race.

14th   Then they will be free men like we
Made in the image of Deity,
Then all of them I trust in God
Will Receive his Gracious word.

15th   Oh what A glorious time twould be
If in Christ all men were free
Heaven and Earth would then Resound
The deads Alive the lost is found

16th   God in Mercy hasten on
       When Mankind Shall all be one
       one in Christ which makes men free
       what A glorious Liberty.
                    Jas. T. Ayers, this Apr 3rd A.D. at 1863,
                         and way down here in Tennessee.

At Gallatin June 16th 63.
Cash on hand..$ 127.00
3 pair shoes at 3.50 per pair...............................   10.50
2 pair suspenders, 1 dollar.................................   2.00
1 vest...   5.50
1 vest...   5.25
1 vest...   4.50
6 packs Envelopes, 20 per pack............................   1.20
1 pack stamped Envelopes..................................   1.00
10 Quires paper   Money made.....................   3.00
Tobacco $321.00..........................   2.75
Duglas...   4.00
Sams nigger   201.10...........................   1.25

Nortons nigger $5.2210..........................   3.10
Jesse Turin 2.00
Plattenburg 2.00

                                                           175.45
                                                          —10.00

     I now owe Peck   5.00   165.45
         and Holsea   5.00   35.65

                         $10.00 $201.10
Pistol cost $17.65
Waɩch cost   18.00

                         35.65
Got Bounty from County...................................   100.00
Paid Gridley...   100.00
Joseph and Henry...   50.00
Squire Beach...   40.00
Cropsey..   25.00
For Sr. kinesses...   4.00
Gave oald Black man......................................   2.00

                                                            321.00

At Gallatin Tenn July 4th 63.
Being sent for into Camp of 129th Ills Reg. I went in Town and made
A Small and Spicy speech to Collered men and Mustered them to the No. of
60 in Ranks. On Tuesday 7th spoke Again and Recvd Authority from Gov
Johnson and General Pain[2] and formed Co. inroled some 80 men. Have
mustered Every day since save Sabbath and now have inroled 120 men.
Have our head quarters South West corner Publick Square at Gallatin in
Big Brick Building this Saturday afternoon July 11th 63.

Jas. T. Ayers

Still in same building and have 149 men this Saturday eve

J. T. Ayers

July 18th 63.
On 16th at night was assalted by Stokes Cavalry[3] and on next morning
also being 17th. No lives lost only one man knocked down.

[A page of the diary contains the following memorandums.]

Selman
Barack
Hildreth
Cann
Banty
Haris
Cable
Hinkle
Titus
Sage
Philips
Curley
Drew
Queen
Cone
Patton
Smith
Carlton

---

[2] Brigadier General Eleazar A. Paine, stationed at Gallatin, guarded the railroad from
Mitchellville to Nashville, Tennessee.

[3] Col. W. B. Stokes was a North Carolinian, loyal to the Union. He joined the Army
in 1862 as colonel of Tennessee cavalry. The race riot noted by Ayers illuminates Governor
Andrew Johnson's opposition to Negro soldiers.

Eleazor Johnston
Burbon Marshall Co. Ia.
6 miles North Lives on yellow River, yellow River Bridge 1 mile North
west of Johnson Road from here to his House.
Mr. David Copelin 74 Ohio Vol, Hope Dale Harison Co. Ohio. This an
inter change with him and me as strangers with understanding to core-
spond.

Aug. 9th 63 at Gallatin
The Amount of goods lef with Olney is thus $29.75

    Orderly serg of Co. E 129 Reg. Ill vol.   J.T. Ayers.

Oct. 2nd A.D. 1863. [*Nashville*]
This day is fine after Raining all day yestarday. Soldiers have been pasing
for two days past on Trains by thousands from the East to Reinforce
Rosecrance. Generals Hooker and Seigle[4] is now her at the St. Cloud
Hotell on there way to Rosey with there Corpse.
God give them good speed.
This 1 O'clock p.m. on Tuesday.   J.T.A.

I write this Oct 22/63 at Nashville Tenn. fine Beautiful day. We have
been here just 2 months this day. No cases in Hospital that are dangerous
and but few there. Boys all well. General Grant[5] was in the Citty and
Left yestarday for Chatanooga and Rosey Left for Cincinnatia. We will
have fun now soon.   J.T. Ayers.

Oct 30th 63 Rainey morning warm and pleasant but muddy withall.
Have sent Letter this morning to Fulwiler, yestarday one to Joseph B.
Ayers.

Lines Coppyed from Nashville press written on the death of A soldier
Boy Diing on Battle the soldier wounded At Gettysburg field.

---

[4] Major Generals of Volunteers William S. Rosecrans, Joseph Hooker, and Franz Sigel.
Rosecrans had been defeated at Chickamauga, September 19-20, 1863. Returning to Chattanooga he was beseiged, and forces from the North were hurried to his relief. Hooker, defeated at Chancellorsville in May, had relinquished command of the Army of the Potomac
to conduct the XI and XII Corps to the Department of the Cumberland. Sigel had commanded
these two corps, but had given up the command in the spring of 1863 on account of bad health.

[5] On October 16, 1863, Grant was given command of the new Military Division of the
Mississippi which included the Departments of the Ohio, the Cumberland, and the Tennessee.
Rosecrans was relieved. Major General of Volunteers George H. Thomas took his place.
With Hooker, Sherman, and Thomas, Grant saved Chattanooga, laid the foundation for his
own appointment as commander in chief, and left the way open for Sherman's Atlanta cam-
paign, which Ayers reported from his modest observation post in 1864.

Nov 4th 63.

A yong soldier Wounded at Gettysburg on being toald by the Surgeon
that he must die Exclaimed with tearful Eyes who will Care for Mother
now,

> Why am I so week and weary,
> So faint my heated breath,
> All Around to me seems dreary,
> Tell me Comrades is this dath.
> Ah how well I know your Answer
> To my fate Ill meekly Bow,
> If youl on tell me truly,
> Who will Care for mother now.
>
> Chorus
>
> Soon with angels Ill be marching
> With Bright Lawrels on my Brow,
> I have for My Country fawlen,
> Who will Care for Mother now,

2nd   Who will Comfort her in sorrow,
> Who will Dry the falen tear,
> Gently Smooth her Wrenkled forehead
> Who will whisper words of cheer,

3rd   Even now I think I see her,
> Kneeling praying for me how,
> Can I leave her in her Anguish,
> Who will Care for Mother now,

3rd   Let this knapsack be my pillow,
> And my mantle be the Sky
> Hasten Comrades to the Battle
> I would Like A soldier dy,
> Soon with Angels Ill be marching
> With Bright Lawrels on my Brow,
> I have for my Country fawlen
> Who will Care for Mother now.

> Chorus soon will angels &.C.

J. T. Ayers, Nov 4th 6[3]

Confound the Luck how sad I Be
Way down here in Tennessee
Sometimes I wish Ide near Been Born
My harts so Sad I feel forlorn

I Read the verse above you see
The orderly does not Agree
he says Confound is not proper
He thinks the word is A whopper.

[*The following poem was revised and used with Ayers' portrait. See frontispiece.*]

heres oald Jimmy sure enough
He Looks oald fashioned Gray and Toughf
Ime sure Camp life is Just the Place
to draw off Jimmys Long slim face.

Nashville, Nov 19th 63
My affairs stand thus
    Cash now $28.50
    Notes and all are
      now   113.75
      J.T. Ayers

Oh God thow cants Save not we
We Cannot gain one victory
Without thy aid and Power
God crown our Efforts for to free
Mankind from Chains and Miserry
And Crush the Traitors power

Thy power to Rule we would confess
We fall at thy feet thy name to bless
In faith we will believe

Oh Joyful day Oh Glorious hope
It Lifts my fainting Spirits up
That in that Holy happy throng
Ill meet my friends before me gon.

A song Composed on the occasion of A Ramble over the incampment of
the 129th Reg Ills Vol, after they had Left at Nashville Tenn.
                        By J.T. Ayers one of its members.

1st   Oh how fleeting and uncertain
      Is the things of time and since
      Past Events are now before me
      All is Drear and in suspence

2nd   Walking ore the oald incampment
      Of the hundred Twenty nine
      How forlorn things seem to whisper
      Boys all gon I left behind.

3rd   What strange stillness seems to whisper
      Round the oald incampment here
      Something whispers mid the silence
      Why should I be in the Rear

4th   What Events Await the Regiment
      Time Can only that Reveall
      (Here I am I A pore oald bachelor)
      Here amid A Land of traitors
      Oh how sad Alone I feel.

5th   Shall I meet those boys Again
      While we Linger on this shore
      Or will war and deadly Combat
      Seperate us Evermore.

6th   Yes we may A while be parted
      Amid the carnage we may fall
      But I hope in Gods good mercy
      Once again to meet them all.

7th   God of mercy grant they blessing
      Send it down upon us all
      Spare us Lord from Rebel bullets
      Spare us Lord for this I call.

                         J.T. Ayers
                  Huntsville Ala Feb 27th 64.

                 MASONIC PROCESSION

      I saw A Band of Brother's Move
      With Slow and Solemn tread
      There Harts ware Joind in tyes of Love
      In Charity ware wed.

2nd   And Types of Light illumed the way
Shone on the Chastning Rod
And in the midst wide open Lay
The gospel of our God.

3rd   I asked A man of four score years
Why after them he Ran
he said And melted into tears
They fed the pore oald man

4th   he said I once was sick and sad
My Lims ware Racked with pain
They Came they Comforted and Clad
The oald man Rose Again

5th   I asked A weeping widow why
She followed those before
She said and wiped her weeping Eyes
They Came unto my doore

6th   They came when all the world beside
Had turned from me and fled
They Came my wants and woes to hide
They gave my Children bread

7th   I Asked an orphant boy why he
His Eager foot steps bends
he said they smile on all like me
They are my Fathers friends

8th   Before he died they Clothed and fed
And all our gifts they gave
And when we wept for Fathers death
They threw gifts in his grave

9th   And such I said Are Masons All
Friends to the needy pore
They never View A brothers fall,
They never Shun his dore

10   And tho tis said they are not free
Virtue and Love and twins
And the best grace of Charity
Hides multitudes of sins.

11   They worship in the Lodge of God
Secret and solemn thare
They bow beneath his sacred Rod
And breath A hartfelt prayer

12   Free masonry Like womans Love
Is taught by Private Rules
So deep that should it publick prove
It would be sport for fools—

The Above I Coppyed from Southern paper at Huntsville Ala. this Apr 29th 64.

UNCLE BENS OALD RAM

1.   Uncle Ben was A quer oald man
A queer Oald man was he
He ownd A Ram A Butting Ram
In fact his butting Propensities prompted
Him to but Every thing he could see

2.   Now Uncle Ben had A fat oald Spouse
A fat old Spouse was She
Who used to feed and pale his cows
That Came up so Regular into the Lawn
Every night and Stood under A Large paretree

3rd.   This fat oald wife near used A Stool
To milk would near sit down
And tho oald Ben Called her A fool
Yet She would never harken to his voice
But to Return the favour She Said he was A clown

4th.   But one sad morn as Brindle Stood
Beneath the Stately Pare
Oald Bens wife in A merry mood
Was milking—occupying her usual position
With her Posterior Extremitys A little Elevated in the air

5th.   The Ram and Ben the fact Espied
And Loudly Ben did Shout
Squat down Squat down he Sturnly cryed
But she did not hear him and before he could interfere
The Ram had turned his fat oald wife inside out

6th. Now uncle Ben was verry wroth
And verry wroth was he
He took the Grindstone from its troughf
And tying A rope to it hung it to an oald partree

7th. Then Like A heavy pendlum
He Swung that mighty Rock
Which Seemed to say Ime up for fun
So Mr. Ram Just Come in will you
And take an Affectionate knock

8th. Right briskly then the fight begun
The Stone would not give in
And Bens oald Ram would yeld to none
So he Butted all day, and when uncle Ben went

9th. to bed he was Still butting Away like all Sin

9th. But when oald Ben Arose next day
And went into the Lawn
The Ram had Butted himself Away
And Every think Else but About two inches
of his tail all was used up completely gon
So I left wondering what queer
things thare are in nature and Rams.

Jas. T. Ayers
Still at Huntsville Ala
Septr 15th, 64.

Haint much to do you may know or I would not of pend this.

FROM THE AJUTANT OF 11TH IOWA TO HIS MOTHER

Just Before the Battle Mother

1st. Just before the battle mother
I am thinking most of you
While upon the field we're watching
with the enemy in view.
Comrades brave Around me lying
Filld with thoughts of home and God
For well they know that on the morrow
Some must Sleep beneath the sod.

Chorus
Farewell mother you may never
Press me to your Hart Again
But Oh you'll not forget me Mother
If I'm numbered with the Slain.

2nd. Oh I long to see you Mother
And the Loveing ones at Home
But I'll never Leave the Banner
Till in Honor I can Come
Tell the Traitors All Around you
That there Cruel words we know
In Every battle kill our soldiers
By the help they Lend the foe.

3rd. Hark I hear the Bugle sounding
Tis the Signal for the fight
And Oh may God protect us mother
As he Ever does the write.
Hear the Battle Cry of freedom
How it swell upon the air
Oh yes we'll Rally Round the Standard
Or We'll perish nobly there.

Foot of Kenshaw Mountain, Georgia, June 26th 64.

JUST AFTER THE BATTLE BY SAME

1st Still upon the field of Battle
I am Lying Mother Dear
With my wounded Comrades waiting
For the morning to Appear
Many Sleep to waken never
In this world of Strife and Death
And many more are faintly Calling
With there feeble Dying breath

Chorus, Mother Dear your Boy is wounded
And the night is Drear with Pain
But Still I feel that I Shall see you
And the Dear oald Home Again.

2nd. Oh the first great charge was fearful
And A thousand Brave men fell
Still Amid the Dredful Carnage
I was Safe from Shot and shell
So Amid the fatal Shower
I had nearly passt the day
When here the dreded minie struck me
And I sunk Amid the fray, Chorus—

3rd Oh the Glorious Cheer of trimph
When the foeman turned and fled
Leaving us the field of Battle
Strewn with Dying and the dead
Oh the torture and the Anguish
That I Could not follow on
But here Amid my falen Comrades
I must wait till Mornings dawn.

Chorus
Mother Dear your Boy is wounded

Kenshaw mountain June 27th 64
Coppyed by J. T. Ayers
Chatanooga Oct. 20eth 64

CAMPAIGN SONG WRITTEN BY J.T.A. AT CHATANOOGA,
OCT. 25th 64.

The Rebs have Tramped down our fields
Destroyed our walls and Ditches,
But Abe Can build our fence Again
And Andy mend the Breeches

Chorus
Lincon is the man we need
Johnson two is handy
Yanky doodle Boys hurrah
For Uncle Abe and Andy

We've got A Grant from Abraham
To beat the Rebels hollow
And when we have A man to Lead
Why we're the Boys to follow.

Oald Butler thinks the way to fight
Is with the gun and Sabre
And doesent see that Contrabands
Are fugitives from Labour

The Copperheads begin to squirm
The Rebs are Looking surley
Sense Sheradin has made them Run
By fighting Late and Early.

And of our Gallant Sherman now
We feel A Little Prowder
Because he's made A lively Hood
By Stirring Rebs with Powder.

Our Country in the Navy two
has many A Brave Defender
There's Faragut knows how to shoot
And make the foe Surrender.

Pore Little Mack has Taught this fact
For which one vote we owe him
Napoleanic Strategy
In Hiding on A Gunboat

We'll have a man for President
Whose Courage never fails him
That Common sense which built the fence
Is Just the thing that Ails him.

IS IT ANY BODDYS BUSINESS

Is it any Boddys business
If A Jentlemen should choose
To wait upon A Lady
If the Lady dont Refuse

Or to Speak A little plainer
That the meaning all may know
Is it any boddys business
If A Lady has A beau.

Is it Any boddys business
When that Jentleman doth call
Or when he Leaves the Lady
Or if he Leaves at all.

Or is it necessary
That Curtain should be Drawn
To save from further Trouble
The out side Lookers on.

Is it Any boddys business
But the Ladys if her Beau
Rideth out with other Ladys
And Dosent mind to Let her know.

Is it Any bodys business
But the Jentlemans if she
Should Except an others Escort
Where Doesent chance to be.

If A person on the side walk
Wether great or wether small
Is it any boddys business
Where that person means to call.

Or if you see A person
While he's calling Anywhere
Is it Any of your business
What his business may be there.

The substance of our query
Simply Stated would be this
Is it Any Boddys business
What an other's business is.

Wether tis or wether tisent
We should Really Like to know
For we're certain if it isent
There are some who make it so.

Coppyed by J.T. Ayers from newspaper scrap thursday Evening sitting
at or in John Waricks House this Nov. 10th A.D. 1864.

1 Fellow soldiers of the Cumberland Loyal brave and true
   Who have Left your Northern firesides Southern traitors to subdue
   Lets send home for A Copperhead A Regular blatant cuss
   And the beauties of A soldiers Life make him share with us.

2 Well put him in A puptent with coald ground for his bed
   With no Rubber blanker under neath no Goverment overhead.
   Let him Shiver thare till morning Sleepless and in pain
   And Each succeeding night should the same thing do again.

3   At breakfast time no dainty dish his appetite would tempt.
     Far from such Dainty Luxurys most soldiers are Exempt
     Sowbelly should he breakfast on, Rusty pore and Black,
     Accompanyd by coffee weak and miserable hard tack.

4   Then preparation quickly make get everything in trim
     March him off on Picket and may A secesh pick at him
     May every bush A Rebel seem strange sounds salute his ears
     And all he sees and all he hears but serve to wake his fears.

5   Let him slosh Round shoeless, in the mud into puddles fall,
     And always Late to dinner be also at bugle call
     While shivering Round the campfire may he burn his boots and close
     May the smoke blow always in his eyes and curl stinging up his nose

6   May he six months without money be and no trusting sutler bout
     And should he get his Canteen filld may it somehow all Leak out
     May he never have A postage Stamp and for his Aching Jaw
     Of tobacco not quiet half Enoughf for even half A chaw.

7   Forced marches may he have to make in Rain and snow and mud
     The driving Rain his clothing soak the chill winds freese his blood
     And that the beauties of A march he might the better see
     Rheumatic twinges all day have and the Chronick dierhea.

8   From Nashville down to Huntsville the Comeing summer days
     Let him hoof it on the dusty Pike beneath the suns hot Rays
     His feet with blisters covered his Lims all weak and Lame
     And I guess hell think a soldiers Life is Anything but tame.

9   Infested may his clothing be with all the Little fry
     That the soil of Allabamma can so Abundantly supply
     Have all his dirty shirts to wash in water scant and black
     Shiftless and Lousy weeks to go no Clean Rags for his back.

10   And when the Conflict Rages fierce keep him always in the front
     Let him feel beside Exposure the battles fiercest brunt
     Let minies whistle Rount his head shrieking sheel burst near
     Let him keenly feel the agonies which Alone the gilty fear

11   And finally in A Hospital minas A leg or so
     Somewhat ematiated and most dredfully low
     Well Lay whats Left of Copperhead upon A dirty bunk
     To Regain his waisted energies on weak tea and tough junk.

12   To the Call of uncle Abraham we Cherfully all flew
     Severed the tyes which bound our Harts bade cherished ones adieu
     And we will not brook the insults which are heaped upon our heads
     By the traitorous northern Cowards the Slimy Copperheads.

I wrote this at Newbern N.C.   Jas. T. Ayers, May 2nd 65
health good Spirits fine.

HOME SPUN DRESS
Air Bonny Blue Flag

1. Oh yes I am A southern girl and glory in the name
   And boast it with fair greater pride than glittiring Wealth or fame
   I envy not the northern girl her Robes of beauty fair
   Tho Dimonds deck her snowey neck and pearls bedeck her hair
   Chorus hurraw huraw for the sunny South so dear
   Thre Chers for the home Spun dress the Southern Ladys ware

2. The homespun Dress is plane I know
         my hats palmetto two
   But then it shows what southern girls
         for southern writes will do
   We scorn to Ware a Dress of Silk
         A bit of Northern Lace
   We make our homespun Dresses up
         And ware them with much grace
         Hurah———

3. Now Northern goods are out of Date
         And since oald Abes Blockade
   We southern girls are quiet content
         With goods our selves have made.
   We sent the Brave from out our Land
         To battle with the foe
   And we will Lend A helping hand
         We Love the South you know
         Hurrah & C———
   Our Land it is A glorious Land
         And ours A glorious Cause
   Then three cheers for the homespun dress
         and for the Southern Boys

4. We sent our sweetharts to the war
         but Dear girls never mind
   The soaldier never will forget
         The girl he left behind
         Hurrah

   A soaldier is the Lad for me
         A brave hart I adore
   And when the Sunny South is free
         And fighting is nomore
   I then will Choose A Lover brave
         From out that glorious band
   The Soaldier boy that I Love best
         Shall have my hart and hand
   So- Hurrah & C

And now yong men A word to you
    If you would win the fair
Go to the field whare Honor calls
    And win your Ladys thare
Remember that our brightest smiles
    Are for the true and brave
And that our tears are for the one
    That fills A soaldiers grave
So Hurrah &C

Jas. T. Ayers.

APPENDIX II

[*This appendix contains clippings which were pasted promiscuously in Ayers' diary, indicating that he originally used the ledger for his accounts and as a scrapbook.*]

JENNY AND THE BERRIES

On a sunny summer morning;
   Early as the dew was dry,
Up the hill I went a berrying;
   Need I tell you—tell you why?
Farmer Davis had a daughter,
   And it happened that I knew,
On each sunny morning,
   Up the hill went berrying too.

Lonely work is picking berries,
   So I joined her on the hill;
"Jenny, dear," said I, "your basket's
   Quite too large for one to fill,"
So, we staid—we two—to fill it,
   Jenny talking—I was still—
Leading where the hill was steep
   Picking berries up the hill.

"This is up hill work," said Jenny;
   "So is life," said I; "shall we
Climb it up alone, or, Jenny,
   Will you come and climb with me?"
Redder than the blushing berries
   Jenny's checks a moment grew,
While, without delay, she answered,
   "I will come and climb with you."

(121)

[The following clipping appears to have been taken from a Huntsville newspaper.]

COMPLIMENTARY

Rev. Dr. Brownlow in the course of a long letter to [t]his paper, dated at this place, after giving an interesting account of his perils by land and tribulations by water in reaching here, speaks as follows of Huntsville and her people.

I have no[w] been in Huntsville four days and nights—could not get away for the breaks on the Railroad—have enjoyed myself finely, and lived well. I have made my head quarters at Gen. Hickman's "Southern Hotel," and visited many friends and new acquaintances. I have been kindly treated by the citizens, irrespective of parties. My old acquaintance Tom White, conveyed me all over the town and vicinity, in a Buggy drawn by a $500 horse, at the rate of eight knots an hour. Hon. Jere. Clemens, and others treated me to a magnificent Oyster Supper. Col. Joe Bradley, the bell-wether of Democracy, and my friends Saunders, the McClung's, Dr. Spotswood, Gen. Bradford, and others, "too-tedious to mention," have called on me. I spoke two hours on Saturday night, to a crowded house, well lighted up with gas. I had to run against an Opera Troupe, in full blast, but I took the crowd, both of gentlemen and ladies. I am not vain, but I think I can compete successfully, with a Circus, and Elephant show, or a theater, in any town in the South!

On Sabbath, I heard Dr. A. R. Erwin preach in the Methodist Church, to a large and attentive audience; and I heard him do what he never fails to do on all such occasions—preach an eloquent, impressive, and number one sermon. At three o'clock I attended one of the African Churches—for there are several here, and witnessed their exercises, while they had some seekers at the altar for prayer. I heard several prayers by old men of color, after Dr. Robinson had concluded his sermon; and in all good conscience, if I were sick, or dying, I would greatly prefer their prayers at my bed side, to those of Henry Ward Beecher, or any of the graceless agitators of the slavery question North of Mason and Dixon's Line!

I took a seat in the family carriage of Mack Brandon, with his elegant little Methodist wife, and niece and rode two miles on the pike where I partook of the finest dinner I have set down to in twelve months.—I have not fully recovered from the effects of the founder yet. On Sabath night

I preached to an over flowing house for Dr. Erwin.—Since then, I have been visiting the children of the Brandons, who were my first acquaintances here, and whose kind treatment in 1829, I have not forgotten. I dined on yesterday, with Mr. Everhart, the Principal of "Bascom Female Institute;" and from seventy to one hundred of the young ladies were at the table, as they board in the College.—It is a splended Institute, with a full corps of competent teachers, and its entire machinery works like the running gear of a clock. Everhart is a graduate of Emory & Henry, and a great man for such a position.

Finally, Huntsville is one of the most thriving, neat and fashionable towns in the South. It has a population of four thousand. Its inhabitants are wealthy, and their dwellings are handsome. The Court House cost about fifty thousand dollars; and the Bank, a stone edifice, is said to have cost a third more. There is a United States Land office here, four churches, Methodist, Episcopalian, Presbyterian, and Cumberland Presbyterian. The Methodists are as numerous as all the rest. There are three newspaper offices, but the best paper published here, is the "Independent," by Wiggs & Dew. Wiggs is a very clever gentleman, and is highly esteemed. His kindness to me I shall not soon forget.

[The next clipping is probably from the same paper.]

AMERICAN INDEPENDENT
PUBLISHED EVERY SATURDAY MORNING
BY WIGGS & DEW
SATURDAY. : : DECEMBER 19, 1857

BROWNLOW'S LECTURE.

Rev. W. G. Brownlow addressed a very large audience in Huntsville on Saturday night last, on the subject of slavery. According to previous determination, he has set out on a tour, which will be continued throughout the present winter and coming spring and summer—remaining in the South during the winter, and proceeding to the North so soon as the dogwood blossoms are visible in the spring. The large audience present were highly pleased with the address, and were convinced of his entire ability to handle the subject and of his being the very man to meet the hypocritical fanatics face to face, and to

"Prove his doctrines orthodox
By Apostolic blows and knocks."

He stated that it was his intention to visit all sections of the South— to see the negroes on the cotton plantations, the sugar plantations, and the rice plantations, immediately before going North, that he might be fully posted, and able to meet the abolitionists and tell them to their faces that they were liars. He would visit the negroes in their cabins in all these sections, and then go among the slavery haters fresh from the scenes of "wo and misery" so feelingly pictured by "old aunt Harriet Beecher Stowe," and her brood of satellites. He would tell them to their faces that they were hypocrites and liars. He would challenge their big men—their freedom-shriekers—to meet him on the stump and to discuss the question fully and fairly. He desired to meet Greely, Theodore Parker, Wendell Phillips, Henry Ward Beecher, Garrison, or any or all of the big guns of anti-slavery, whom he would denounce as infidels, as slanderers, as hypocrites, as liars, and as God-forsaken wretches generally, and would prove to all honest, right-thinking men that they were such.

Greely had proposed that when Dr. B. arrived in New York, he should be met and his argument refuted by Fred Douglass, a negro orator. Said he was prepared to meet Fred's case; that he intended to take with him a negro from Knoxville, a slave, known as Alf Anderson, who should meet and discuss the subject with Fred. Said Alf was a large, fine looking negro—reads and writes well—had some experience as a public speaker— being in the habit of addressing his colored brethern on the subject of temperance—a strong, forcible speaker—rather eloquent than otherwise— a native of East Tennessee. He would meet all their colored orators— advocate and illustrate Southern slavery, and oppose abolitionism. And, in the mean time, if they could induce Alf to go with them upon an underground railroad to Canada, or to remain in their glorious land of freedom, he would offer no opposition, but let them steal him if they could.

To Greeley's proposition, he said that, as a Southern gentleman, he could not meet Fred, because of the color of his skin; still he thought there was not a free negro north of Mason & Dixon's Line, who was not as honerable, and every way as worthy of confidence, as any Black Republican editor, politician or preacher in all that ungodly region.

He said he had no confidence in the politician or the divine at the North who was engaged in this villainous agitation of the slavery question. There were true, reliable, conservative men at the North, and here in the South, who came from the North, but they were not among these graceless agitators, nor did they approve either their doctrines or policy. Said if he found any of their vagabond philanthropists in heaven, where he hoped to go after death, he should believe they got into that world of bliss and purity by practicing a fraud upon the door-keeper!

The Doctor was particularly hard upon the Northern portion of the Methodist Church. Said he had been among them, and knew them well. Said the clergy among them would enter their fine churches on the Sabbath day, and preach *feelingly* against the sin of slavery, and shed burning tears over the oppressions of the "servile progeny of Ham" in the Southern States—their membership would respond in tears to the harrangues of their pastors, and on the next day, in a business transaction they would cheat a Southern slave out of the pewter that ornamented the head of his walking stick!

But we have not space to give even as synopsis of the address, nor did we take notes to do so. The speech was a forcible one, and exceedingly appropriate. The speaker proved from the Scriptures that our Saviour recognized slavery, and that it was an institution which existed and had been recognized by God from time immemorial. He approved the traffic in slaves, but opposed a repeal of the laws prohibiting the African slave trade. Showed that before the enactment of this law, the trade was carried on almost exclusively by the people of the New England States, and that even since its enactment, slave vessels have every year been fitted out in Northern ports, manned with Northern men, who continue to steal slaves from Africa, at the risk of being taken as pirates; that the Southern States were indebted to the pious Yankees for the slaves they now have—the Yankees having *stole* and *sold* them into slavery.

The speaker was opposed to a dissolution of the Union. He preferred to remain in the Union, and fight those who desired to encroach upon our rights, rather than secede, and give up our interest in the National Treasury, the Navy, and the Government property generally; believed that the warmblooded Southerners, in defence of their rights, could whip the cold, calculating Abolitionists five to one. He thought it better to whip sense into them, than to secede from them.

He complimented the New School Presbyterians for their late action in withdrawing from the fanatical portion of that church.—Thought the Episcopalians were making a good move in the right direction, in establishing a University in the South.

The speaker wound up his speech in an eloquent appeal in behalf of the Union of the South against the common enemy—the abolitionists — which called forth loud and repeated cheers from the audience.

[*The source of the next clipping is unknown.*]

MILDLY JUDGE YE OF EACH OTHER

(We gather the following gem of Christian sentiment from the fields of poesy, and hope its blessed teachings may not pass unimproved:)

> Mildly judge ye of each other,
>   Be to condemnation slow;
> The very best have got their failings,
>   Something good the worst can show.
> The brilliant sun hath spots of darkness
>   On its radiant front, they say;
> And the clock that never goeth,
>   Speaks correctly twice a day.
>
> Do not mock your neighbor's weakness,
>   When his random whims you see;
> For, perhaps, he something like it
>   Every day beholds in thee.
> Folly leavens all our natures;
>   Soundest metal hath its flaws,
> And the rigid stoic scorner
> Is no wiser for his saws.
>
> Every mortal hath his hobby;
>   It may foolish seem to you,
> But, remember, bright or simple,
>   You have got your hobby, too.
> Let a fellow-feeling warm you,
>   When you criticise your friend;
> Honor virtues in his actions,
> In yourself his vices mend.
>
> Think not those whom mortals honor
>   Are the best the earth affords;
> For no tongue of praise doth blazon
>   Forth the deeds which God rewards.
> There are fish behind in ocean;
>   Good as ever from it came;
> And there are men, unknown, as noble,
>   As the laurel'd heir of fame.

[The following clipping evidently appealed to Ayers, also.]

On Wednesday morning, May 4th, a meeting of ladies of the various evangelical denominations of the city was held at Concert Hall, Philadelphia, for the purpose of adopting measures for the organization of Ladies' Christian Commissions in the various churches throughout the country.

The Rev. Bishop Simpson, of the Methodist Episcopal church, Philadelphia, was called to the chair, and Rev. Edward Lounsberry, of the Episcopal church, appointed-Secretary. Rev. J. Addison Henry, of the Presbyterian church led in prayer; after which Rt. Rev. Chas. P. McIlvaine, D.D., Bishop of Ohio, and Rev. Robt. J. Parvin, of Philadelphia addressed the meeting. These gentlemen were followed by the Rev. Dr. Kirk, of the Congregational church, Boston, who delivered the following address:

ADDRESS OF REV. DR. KIRK.

Sisters in Christ:—Permit me, before introducing the subject specifically under the consideration of this meeting, to make a general suggestion in regard to the times in which we are living. The child of God should be more patriotic and loyal than others, should feel the nation's woes and perils with peculiar sensitiveness. Yes, the Christian, of all men, should feel his little barque tossing on the tempestuous sea which threatens the destruction of his country. But that feeling of solicitude and sorrow should in him be tempered and modified by another. He can neither sorrow nor fear as those who have no hope in God. He has confidence that God's providence is moving the world forward, and not backward. He has no fears for himself; for he will outlive society and its institutions; and his home is in "the city that hath foundations, whose builder and maker is God."

There was a woman, who, whatever she was or was not, whatever she did or failed to do, had made up her mind to love Jesus her Redeemer with her whole heart. Nothing was too precious to give him; no expression of love or gratitude to him could be extravagant. But what could she do? There were no rules laid down by the church to guide her. There were no recognized models for her to imitate. What then did she do? She consulted her own heart, and that told her what to do. But there was, after all, no great value in the act she did perform. The Lord indeed made a kindly interpretation of it, when he said that she had done this for the day of his burial. But it had no real value to that direction, for God was not to suffer his Holy One to see corruption. Let us then look at the act, and his sentence pronounced upon it when it was censured. This woman purchased an alabaster-box of costly perfume, and carried it to the house where Jesus was entertained at a supper. Breaking the box, she poured the precious contents on his sacred person, washing his feet with her grateful tears, and wiping them with her hair.

When Jesus heard the cold, cynical, selfish grumbler object to the action, what was his reply? A precious sentence: "She hath done what she could." That is enough, humble, obscure, diffident sister. To meet his approval, you are not to seek nor gain that of any other; you are not to imitate or equal any other; you are not necessarily even to escape the censure of others. Do what you can for Christ.

But who is to measure your ability? One who, for your sake, exchanged a throne for a gibbet; who, to secure your life, gave himself to death; one who thoroughly reads the heart; one who requires no brilliant display of affection, but rightly interprets a tear or a sigh; who puts a high value upon a little box of ointment, an unobserved desire to touch only the hem of his robe, a cup of cold water given in his name, or two mites thrown into his treasury.

BUT, WHAT CAN YOU DO?

What can the weakest or obscurest do? First of all, you can love your Redeemer, and consecrate yourself to his service. He is worthy of all, and infinitely more than you can render. Give it to him, all the wealth and strength of your love and confidence. Give him the first place, and then every human being can have its proper place. Live in him; live for him.

Love to our Lord and Saviour should always, but especially in this day of rebuke and chastisement, take on the form of humility. The divine injunction is: "Humble yourselves under the mighty hand . . . It is a hand so broad you cannot escape from...;" so "mighty," you cannot successfully resist its pressure. Struggling and fretting but increase the pain. Submit; that is our duty and our policy. Go down. How low? Until you reach the other hand; for "underneath are the everlasting arms." And the aim of infinite goodness is simply this to [*illegible*] until there is nothing but God to lean upon. We must go down through creatures and idols and our own strength, until we touch the supporting hand—then the crushing hand will cease its pressure. This is the method of infinite love, when it has purposed our highest good. But, will he not sink me, or the beloved institutions of my country, and with them the hope of the world, into the abyss? No; he is jealous of your confidence, and desires to be its supreme object. Humble yourselves in this day of your country's calamity. If the Ninevites could consent to fast, and clothe themselves in sackcloth at the call of a strange prophet, surely the Christian women of the Republic can consent to express a sympathy with their suffering and imperilled country, by self denial in dress and food; by simplicity in both, to give outward and appropriate expression to their grief for sins which have so provoked their beloved Reedeemer, and called forth from him such expressions of displeasure.

To put it on the lowest ground, it is in bad taste to increase the splendor of dress and furniture, and the luxury of living, when our country, as dear to us as our kindred, lies sick unto death.

And this leads me to show another good thing each of you can do. Love your country, and judge the character of others in part, by their regard for it. Love your country; and willingly sacrifice anything its interests demand. If economy in dress and living will affect the value of our currency, and tend to save the financial credit of the Government, let there be no hesitation. If Southern women will dress in calicoes for such a Government as their leaders are seeking to establish, surely Northern women can do as much for our Government. Love your country. It is worthy of your love. None ever was more so. Its institutions, its national character, its relations to the human race, and its coming history, its relations to the church of Christ, all claim for it a high place in our affections. Bear its sorrows on your heart. Regard it as you do a sick child, with a never interrupted sympathy; carrying its pain into your ver sleep with you.

Indentify yourself with the soldier who is defending that country. It matters not who the man is that occupies that sacred post; for the time being, and as such, place him in your inner heart. Count his family yours, so as to share with them their sorrows and solicitudes.

You cannot over-estimate the power of your sex in certain directions. It seems to me that one of the strongest forces in this rebellion is, the devotion of the women of the Southern States to what they call their country and its cause. Blind, misguided and wicked as it is, yet, like the Satan of Milton, it is admirable in its energy and self-sacrificing persistency. It has been said that the shrewd plotters of this villany if rightly estimating this power, took care in their chosen mates to fire the hearts of the Southern women; that Mr. Brooks was by them goaded on to make his brutal attack on Mr. Sumner. And we saw in the early history of the war, how powerful was the stimulus of their zeal on the hearts of sons and brothers, husbands and friends. We hear of the richest of them at this day suppressing the desire of dressing according to their taste and ability, that they may have the means of ministering to their starving soldiers. In itself this is noble. And shall not the women of the North at least equal them, if not surpass them in this?

Might not every lady send a letter to the army every month; not only to kindred there, but to friends, or even strangers? The times and circumstances would remove from it every shade of impropriety. Ascertain if any young man from your neighborhood is without friends, or if a family find it difficult to write frequently to the husband and father. Be in such cases the amanuensis for all your loyal sisters, and frequently write a letter to such. Tell them about home, tell them about their neighbors. Be cheerful even entertaining in your communications. Put not a line of disaster or fear in them. Be kind, and above all, let them see that you are chiefly anxious for their eternal welfare. You may have heard much said about the value of letters to a soldier; but you cannot overestimate it.

Pray for your country, the government, the army, and the navy.

Sisters, do you know how wonderful, how glorious a reality is prayer! Have you searched the Scriptures to see what a channel of the divine power God has been pleased to make it?

But what is prayer? It is the heart, not the head, uttering itself to God. It is the soul, pleading in the name of Christ, for great blessings which God alone can bestow. Wherein lies its power? In these elements, desire, humility, confidence, thankfulness. Specific and strong desiring is the essence of prayer; always consenting to be refused, always preferring God's will to its own; yet specific and earnest in desiring. This comparison was once made in my hearing; a mother, passing a room where her children were playing, heard one of them crying. But the quick instinct of a mother's heart told her the child was not grieved. It was play-cry. Repassing the room she heard another cry. This turned her step quick as though[t] to the sufferer. That was a real cry; a heart-tone was in it. Too often we have play-cry. When our hearts are burdened and grieved, there is a Father's ear quick to hear it.

Mark that child climbing up to its father's lap, throwing its little arms around his neck. Tell me if that is not a position of power. He may be a man whose will sways the mind of a nation, on whose eloquence that nation waits for impulse and guidance. But in the strong language of Scripture, that child takes hold upon the strength of that strong man. Such is prayer. Except ye be converted and become as little children, ye have no power in prayer.

Pray, sisters; pray for your country, for the men who guide it and the men who defend it. Be simple, be earnest, be humble, be bold with a holy "boldness to enter into the holiest by the blood of Jesus!" "With thanksgiving let your request be made known in the name of Jesus."

All this you certainly can do, whatever station you occupy, however limited the gift entrusted to you by the Lord, who accepts "according to what man hath."

Now, let me suggest to you one other course of action. Do what you can to sustain the Christian Commission. You know its work and its claims. None of all the funds of Christian beneficence is, for the time, paramount to it.

And we now propose to you a course which, while severely taxing no individual, will secure immense results. Within your own parish see to it that a society be organized, if agreeable to the officers and members of the church, to secure a yearly subscription in money, and such labor for the army as the Central Committee, from time to time, may show to be needed for furnishing the soldiers with hospital garments. See to it that while the necessity for this kind of effort shall continue your association be kept in vigorous operation.

And when your account is made by him whose favor is life, may it be "She hath done what she could."

Remarks were also made by Rev. J. E. Chesshire, of the Baptist church, Rev. A. G. McAuley, of the Reformed Presbyterian church, Rev. Dr. Newton, and Rev. R. G. Matlack of the Episcopal church.

Rev. J. G. Maxwell read the following resolutions, which were unanimously adopted:

Resolved, As the unanimous expression of the sentiment of this meeting that we recommend to ladies of the various Evangelical churches in the loyal States, that they organize ladies' Christian Commissions in each congregation, auxiliary to the United States Christian Commission.

Resolved, That the United States Christian Commission be requested to issue a circular embodying a form of organization with hints as to the process of organizing.

Resolved, That we recommend that the terms of membership for these auxiliaries be fixed at $1 per annum.

FORM OF CONSTITUTION FOR LADIES' CHRISTIAN COMMISSIONS, WITH SUGGESTIONS.

To carry out the National plan of Ladies' Christian Commissions fully, it will be necessary, 1. To form a Commission in each separate congregation. 2. To have each Commission directly auxiliary to the United States Christian Commission or some one of its branches. 3. To have the organization reported in full to the United States Christian Commission, or the Branch with which the Ladies' Commission connects itself, together with the name of the *Ladies' Commission* and the *names of the officers*. 4. To have the amount paid in for admission fees paid over directly to the United States Christian Commission or the Branch.

[*Poems appealed to Ayers. It is not surprising to find this one in his scrapbook.*]

DOWN BY THE RAPIDAN.

By Emma Garrison Jones.

How, like a dream of childhood, the sweet
    May-day goes by!
A golden brightness gilds the air, a rose-
    blush paints the sky;
And the Southern winds come bearing in
    their freights of rare perfume
From the far-off country valleys, where
    the Spring-flowers are in bloom.

We sit beneath our windows, and watch
    the evening sun,
And count the silver rain drops, desending
    one by one.
The very town seems silenced in a soft,
    delicious calm
How different is the scene to-night down
    by the Rapidan!

Down by the rushing Rapidan, hark!
    how the muskets crack!
The battle-smoke rolls up so thick, the very
    heavens are black.
No blossom-scented winds are there, no
    drops of silver rain;
The air is thick with sulphurous heat, and
    filled with morns of pain.

Oh! let us not forget them, our brave,
    unselfish boys,
Who have given up their loved ones, their
    happy household joys,
And stand to-night in rank and file, deter-
    mined to a man,
To triumph over treason, down by the
    Rapidan!

And let our hearts be hopeful; our faith
    unwavering, strong;
Right must be all-victorious when battling
    with the *Wrong*.
Let us bear up our heroes hands! Pray,
    every soul that can,
"God bless our boys who fight to-night
    down by the Rapidan!"

Washington, May 12, 1864.

[*The next clipping probably was used by Ayers in his sermons.*]

"I AM BUT A LITTLE CHILD."

By S. V. R. Ford.

"**I am but a little child**: I know not how to go out or come in" I Kings 3:7.

"I am but a little child,"
Weak and easily beguiled,
Foes without and strifes within
Tempt my little heart to sin.
Look in pity, Lord, on me;
Let me trust alone in thee;
Let me on thy bossom rest,
Clasp me to thy loving breast.

If, forgetting thee, I stray
Into sin's enticing way,
Leave me not to perish there
In the tempter's cruel snare.
When I'm tempted to digress
From the path of righteousness,
Let me hear thy Spirit say,
"Little child, 'This is the way.' "

When in danger I shall be,
Let me quickly fly to thee,
Trusting in thy mighty arm,
Nought my tender soul shall harm.
If I faint or weary grow,
If I suffer pain or woe,
Let thy strength my portion be,—
Still sustain and comfort me.

Daily as I older grow,
May I more of Jesus know;
Meekly learning at his feet
Wisdom's lessons pure and sweet.
Let me have his blessed mind;
Make me gentle, meek, and kind:
Let my words and actions tell
That I love my Saviour well.

With a meek and patient mind,—
With a loving heart, and kind,—
With a temper sweet and mild,
Though "I'm but a little child,"
Christ will be my constant friend,
He will keep me to the end;
He will take me when I die
To my home beyond the sky.

INDEX

(135)